The Camp: Stories from the Summer

By Aaron Conn

This 2nd edition was published in 2014.

TABLE OF CONTENTS

Intro to the 10th Anniversary Edition 4

Intro from Author 6

The Camp: Vocab and Terms 8

Bunkmates and Counselors In *The Camp* Series 10

The Early Years: 1991-2004...14

The Camp: Season 1 16

7th Grade and the first half of the summer (2004-2005)..23

The Camp: Season 2 24

8th grade (2005-2006) 32

The Camp: Season 3 33

The Camp: Season 4 52

The Camp: Season 5 84

Tim Kedge: A Wise Man (1949-2009)...125

The Camp: Season 6 128

Introduction to the revisits 173

The Camp: Season 1 Revisited 174

The Camp: Season 2 Revisited 184

Counting Out Time: Days and Dates From *The Camp* 194

Acknowledgements 203

Remembering Tim Kedge..204

Intro to the 10th Anniversary Edition

Hello,

What you are holding in your hands (or looking at on your e-reader, for those of you who don't miss the feeling of holding an actual book) is the 10th Anniversary Edition of *The Camp: Stories from the Summer*. I know what you're asking right now: "Aaron, how the hell is this the 10th Anniversary Edition when the book came out in 2010?"

First off, I will commend you on knowing that this book was self published in 2010. That impresses me! Seriously: the reason why this is the 10th Anniversary Edition is because July 2014 marks 10 years since I first started going to Summit Camp. I feel that something like this is worth celebrating.

So what's different in this edition? Well, there are a couple of things. I've finally figured out how to resize a document in Word so you'll see that the text takes up the entire page (at least that's what I want it to do). I've also added page numbers. I was unable to do this before because these were all Word files being uploaded to Lulu. I don't think there was a way to add page numbers, even though I wanted them. I was able to do it this time by having the entire book in one Word document.

Another change I've made is the overall structure of the paragraphs. All the essays are the same and remain unchanged, but the problem I had when writing these essays was not knowing when to end a paragraph. It hurts my eyes looking at those huge clusters.

The only thing that has changed in the essays (specifically Seasons 3 and 4) is the addition of footnotes. Now, why on earth would I need footnotes for a book like this? As I read the essays now, there are some parts that make me cringe. Someone might take a sentence the wrong way or may not understand something. I told myself I wouldn't do revisits of Season 3 through 6 because they would be too long. I didn't want to add or change the writing either. So I've added footnotes, which act more as a commentary that you'd get on a DVD for a movie.

Aside from these things, everything else has stayed the same. I do have to get one thing straight: I do mention in the book that I envisioned my journal entries as a reality show, and that the essays would do the same. After writing and reading these essays, they do not come across as a reality show. Even if I wanted to, reality television just doesn't translate into a book. What I've created instead is a collection of essays, written within the span of almost five years. In doing so, you will probably notice a growth in my writing- which shows that I'm growing as a person too.

Enjoy my book…

Aaron Conn
February 25, 2014

Intro from Author

What you are about to read is a story that spans over five years and six summers. I call it *The Camp*. These are the essays I wrote about each year based on journals I kept each year. The essays were all written about five months after a year ends. As you read, you will see a growth in my writing. Despite some spelling errors, I hope you get the feel of all of my essays. I was thirteen when I wrote the first one. For Seasons 5 and 6, I wrote the essays for them shortly after I came back those years. I've also revisited the first two seasons. Some of my essays had to be cleaned up for bad language. I'm aware I have my freedom of speech but there is such a thing when we abuse that freedom.

What makes my experience at camp different from everyone else's? Nothing really but there is one difference: all of the campers at my camp, Summit Camp, have learning disabilities and the other things that come with it. The camp was also kosher, which kept us from eating most things. Everything I say in these essays is the truth. I kept very good journals and from what I'm told, I have a hell of a memory.

I hope you enjoy reading my essays.

Aaron Conn

PS: Please note that everything I say is the truth. All the events have happened and all the people in them do exist. Just to be safe, I've given all my former bunkmates new names. Their names aren't that different as the first letter of their new name is the first letter of their real name. I do this for everyone except Max and Patrick. As for my counselors, the names are real. I will never mention their last names just for their safety.

<u>Timeline of writings</u>
Season 1: Written in January-April 2005 at 13 years old
Season 2: Written in January-April 2006 at 14 years old
Season 3: Written in March or April 2007 at 15 years old
Season 4: Written in early January 2008 at 16 years old
Season 5: Written in late August 2008 at 16 years old
Season 6: Written in late August 2009 at 17 years old
Season 1 revisit: Written in March 2009 at 17 years old
Season 2 revisit: Written in October or November 2009 at 18 years old

The Camp: Vocab and Terms

I know for sure there'll be readers who have no idea what I'm talking about. This should clear things up as I explain the meanings of things at Summit.

Bunk stars- The bunk star system is one of discipline. In each period, bunks had the opportunity to earn up to four bunk stars. The four stars were for four different areas: listening, safety, helpfulness, and being respectful. On every Friday, the stars would be added up and announced at dinner for both lower and upper camp.

Canteen- Like most camps, Summit has a canteen. The canteen is a place where snacks are kept. The snacks could be for a reward or for evening activity. The canteen mostly has tofu ice cream and soda. The canteen is also a place to hang out. There were tables to sit at and there were arcade games to play.

Horseshoe Time- Horseshoe time is after dinner and it's pretty much a free period. You can do whatever you want (except stay in the cabin) and get to connect with people outside of your bunk. Sometimes, you can be rewarded and go to the computer lab during this time or play a game with a friend. The possibilities are endless with Horseshoe.

ST and GST program- ST stands for "super teen". The ST program is for the older kids on Summit. So instead of being a B bunk (boy bunk) or a G bunk (girl bunk), they are in a ST bunk (teenage boy bunk) or a GST bunk (teenage girl bunk). STs also get to make money both in waitering or for a job of their choice. Three days into the year, campers get to pick what they would like to help in. Once everyone is taken care of, campers are given schedules for their work periods. An ST camper can make up to $24 in one week. This money is given on trip day so you can spend it.

ST/GST socials- Socials are basically dances at a school. Every Saturday, STs and GSTs can socialize with others outside of their bunk. You can dance to the music playing in the Rec Hall or you can bring something to do.

Tribes- Tribes is a special period for bunk counseling. In other words, it's group therapy except it can be fun. You can play plenty of "getting to know you" games. Tribe sessions are held by people in the SITs. SITs are people who act as mentors and one of them will lead one tribe session. From Seasons 3 to 5, Julie was our mentor.

Bunkmates and Counselors in *The Camp* Series

<u>Season 1 (2004)</u>
Aaron
Alec
Andrew
Brandon
Byron
Jaron
Kyle
Trent

Jeff, Nathan, Kenda
Tom
Danelle

<u>Season 2 (2005)</u>
Aaron
Alec
Brandon
Colin
Jim
Kyle
TJ
Trent
Jimmy

Jono, Kelvin, Kayla
Brian
Karli

<u>Season 3 (2006)</u>

Aaron
Brandon K.
Colin
Kyle
Nolan
Mitch
Max
Mark
Patrick
Zeke
Elliot
Trent

Carl, Tsur, Alex
Paul
Neale

Season 4 (2007)
Aaron
Brandon H.
Brent
Byron
Colin
Joel
Kyle
Nolan
Noah
Mark
Patrick
Brandon G.
Drake
Joe
Kevin
Max

Stuart

Carl, Chris, Bekka, Sammie-Jo
Simon, Craig
Neale

Season 5 (2008)
Aaron
Aldan
Brandon G.
Glenn
Joseph W.
Joel
Kevin
Max
Seth S.
Ernie
Jed
Jerry
Liam
Ruben
Tim

Carl, Simon, Carol
Jon
Neale

Season 6 (2009)
Aaron
CJ
Byron
Eli
Joseph K.
Joe

Max
Otto
Seth M.
Aden
Billy
Isaac
Mark M.
Nolan
Noah
Seth
Alison
Sierra

Gary, Dawson, Nicole, Terra
Carl
Pete, Christine

The Early Years: 1991-2004

I was born on October 23, 1991. From what I've been told, I was a very happy child and also very hyperactive. I was also a bit slower than most of my peers. My parents found out that I had ADHD. I also had extreme case of anxiety. For kindergarten and first grade, I went to Mullica Hill Friends School. The school was a Quaker school but it was the only one that I was accepted for that had full day kindergarten. When my parents learned that there would be only one teacher starting in second grade and on, they decided I needed extra help. So I left Friends and was left without a school.

It's law that kids are supposed to go to the school that is closest to them. However, that school didn't have what I needed: in-class support (in other words, two teachers in the classroom). With the help of my old pre-school (who took kids from kindergarten to fifth grade to three different schools), I went to Loring Flemming from second to fifth grade. I enjoyed Loring Flemming. By the age of nine, I began learning more about a band called the Beatles. I became fascinated in them and started listening to their music and learning about them.

In June 2001, my dad suddenly passed away. To this day, no one knows how he went. He just got sick and died. It hurt me a lot. I knew very well that after I was done with fifth grade in 2003, I would be going to the middle school closest to me. I was the only fifth grader from Loring Flemming going to Ann Mullen Middle School in 2003. I wasn't completely on my own: my former fourth grade teacher happened to be my homeroom teacher and mentor. Still, I found it hard to make friends and keep up with the constant changes. As my sixth grade year started to wind down, I knew my mom had signed me up for some special sleep-away camp called Summit Camp. The camp, from what I was told, consisted entirely of boys and girls who had learning disabilities. I was worried.

14

Ever since I finished kindergarten, I was going to a day camp ironically called Great Times Day Camp. When I was younger, I loved it. The concept of going to camp and then returning home the same day thrilled me. However, I didn't have too many friends. I was pretty hyper for those first few years. By 2004, my seventh year was absolute hell. No one talked to me nor did anyone give a crap about me. I remember coming home from my last day there crying: I hated this place. I never wanted to come back. Week by week, I grew more and more anxious about Summit Camp. Then I came up with a brilliant idea.

My brilliant idea was to keep a journal during the four weeks I would be at this place. I would document day after day and write about how awful it was and how I was going to cry myself home. It was perfect. Due to my love for reality shows like *Survivor* and *The Apprentice*, I imagined this camp thing as a reality show. If this was a reality show, what would I call it? After thinking about how simple reality show titles were then, I decided to call it *The Camp*. When I told my mom, she replied,

"That's it?"

I did feel it needed something a little more creative but *The Camp* just stayed with me. I didn't know that it would occupy the next six summers and five years of my life

The Camp: Season 1
By Aaron Conn

I never wanted to go to sleep away camp. I was afraid of being away from my parents. Now in 2004, my mom signed me up for Summit Camp, a special camp for kids with learning disabilities or social skill problems. I didn't want to go but I had a great time! Here is my story of what happened during those 27 days.

It was July 27th, 2004. I was going to a hotel where vans would come and take me to Summit Camp. I was nervous. I was with my mom and my dad's mother. Once I got on the van and said goodbye to my mom and grandma, I started to cry a little. I told the van driver of my worries and he said he'd keep an eye on me. I was fine so I out got my CD player and listened to two Kiss albums, *Kiss* and *Hotter Than Hell*. We got there and I met Kenda. I met Kenda before during the tour of the camp. She said hi and we talked. Did I mention it was raining? Yeps. Anyways, Kenda and I got to the cabin and showed me where I would sleep. Then, Kenda and I went to the computer lab, where my new bunkmates were. Like I said, it was raining so we all went to the cabin. I met Nathan and said hello. I told him that I was getting nervous and he said I'd be fine. I sat on my bed, watching everyone.

I took out my CD player and got my CDs. All of a sudden, the bunk noticed my collection and were saying things like "Wow!" Two of these people were Andrew and Jeff. Jeff was one of my counselors, who I would soon know very well. Andrew was a bunkmate and had the same music interests as me. Long story short, we soon got to the dining hall and had spaghetti. I started to get nervous and "homesick". Tom, who slept in our cabin but wasn't our counselor, asked

"Are you homesick?"

I nodded. He basically said that I would have a good time. Soon after, it was Horseshoe Time. Horseshoe Time is when all the camp walks around the camp and talk to other people. The main office has a field that's in the shape of a horseshoe. So, that took about 20 minutes. After that was the evening activity. Tonight was movie night! The movie we watched was *Billy Madison* with Adam Sandler. It was funny! After movie night was over, we went back to the cabin. We had a kid named Byron before who wasn't respected well. He was out and along came Trent. Trent came in and got to his new bed. Soon after, we went to bed. I did have trouble sleeping that night.

I woke up on Day 2 to see that my bed's opening was covered with Kyle's sleeping bag. Kyle also had dropped his glasses on my bed. This may sound weird but I remember Kyle from a day camp I used to go to. We got along very well but then all of a sudden, I didn't see him anymore. Here I am reunited with him along with five other boys including Andrew, Brandon, Trent, Alec, and Jaron. That day was very good. We had breakfast, swimming tests, and my first shower in the cabin. I was very nervous about this but I came up with a plan that would continue throughout the year. I would go in a stall, put a towel around me and then my bathrobe. I'd come out and then go in one of the showers. As a result, Trent and I became the only kids in B12 to not "flash"! We also waitered on this day.

Day 3 was pretty good. We saw *Spiderman 2* and had talent night. Day 4 was good also but Kenda was sick. This was the day that it became official that I was an all star as I did great in every period. Jeff got to know me more this day and I also told him about my dad's passing. Day 5 was also good. Keiyoshi from B13 came to sub for Jeff. One of the most classic moments was about to happen

17

in…a stall. Yes! I went to the bathroom and Keiyoshi was in the other. He started to make noises. After he was done, he said

"That was a very good pee."

Kenda returned on Day 6, when I had a tooth ache. Day 7 was very fun. We went on a hiking trip all day long and then went to Pizza Hut.

Day 8 was pretty cool. We went on yet another trip. This trip was a canoeing trip. I wanted to be with Andrew and Trent because I had gotten along with them very well. The rule was that three people had to be in a canoe and one of those three people had to be a counselor. I ended up with Jeff and Brandon, who I would soon get along with.

Something funny happened during this trip. I asked Jeff who were those people near the lake and what were their names. He said their names were Cleopatra, Theodore, and Floyd. On that day, it was declared that I had killed Floyd. I don't know why but while everyone was swimming, I was talking to Trent. Later that day, we saw the rest of *Billy Madison* and watched some of *School Of Rock*.

Day 9 was pretty crazy. Kyle had wanted to listen to my downloaded stuff which included a Spongebob song. He says "Aaron, look". He pulled down his pants and…you get the picture. Not only that but Alec also pulled down his pants but this time, everyone in Danelle's unit saw it.

That same day, we ate lunch on the tennis court. I was with Trent, Andrew, and Cooper and Alex of B10. We were talking about our musical interests. This was the problem. Trent, Andrew, Cooper and I liked classic rock. Alex was into hip hop like Britney Spears, Jojo, and the list goes on. The funny thing is that he didn't know any of the bands we were talking about. That night, we watched the rest of *School Of Rock* since we were going to be doing a show on it.

18

Day 10 would have to be one of the best days. It was trip day and we were going to the mall. I only had $5 which my dad's mother, had given me before I left. Of course, I wanted to get an album. The camp gives us an extra $6. After doing the math, I have a total of $11. The groups were CHOSEN by counselors. I wanted to be with Andrew, Trent, Brandon, or Kyle. I didn't mind being with Alec or any of my counselors. I ended up with Nathan and Jaron. I liked Nathan. He's a very nice person but Jaron was someone I didn't know well enough. He suggested that we all buy a cell phone.

I had gotten a Kiss album, *Hot In The Shade* and a chocolate ice cream from Dairy Queen. Karaoke night was wild that night!!!

It was still week 2 and so much was going on. Day 11 and 12 seem to have gone by quickly but on Day 11, we saw a play with Beatles music in it. On Day 13, we went biking. I also had gotten some sad news: Rick James died. I wasn't totally shocked but I was sad to hear it. There was also Hockey night and we lost against B11. I think the reason why we lost is because Jaron and I missed the ball. The bunk was not angry at me but they were all angry at Jaron. It's just a game!!!

Day 14 was Track And Field Day. It was like color war but with three colors: red, white, and blue. I hate sports. My main interest is in music and I just don't like playing sports. I don't mind Soccer and Hockey but any other sport, I don't think I'm good at. I'd like to thank the Lord that I had twisted a muscle and I couldn't do everything.

On Day 15, we watched *50 First Dates*. Day 16 was good but the night wasn't so great. We were going to sleep in the canteen. We could have canteen treats and use tents to sleep in or sleep in front of them. Of course, I was with Andrew and Trent in one tent. We were going to watch a movie. It was between *Nutty Professor II* and *Hellboy*. I wanted to go to sleep with laughs and not bad images. So,

I voted for *Nutty Professor II*. After a 4-3 vote, *Nutty Professor II* won. I went back to my tent and Trent would not let me in saying

"I thought you were one of us" and stuff like that.

Andrew said "Trent, just let him in."

I was happy that I was back in my tent but just with Andrew. Trent had gone off in front of the tent. I was hurt. I thought he absolutely hated me. I talked to all of my counselors and told them what had happened and how I felt. Nathan said that Trent would forget about it in the morning and everything would be fine. I agreed with him and went to sleep.

On Day 17, we went to a fair. It was raining! I was very lucky to be with Andrew and Jeff. I didn't go on anything but bought some food. We also joined Adam, MJ, and Andrew of B13. Something funny happened while we were ordering food. Adam (counselor) asked about the sizes for the french fries. The lady said that this was the small and that was the medium. He says,

"Wow, I can really see the difference."

Day 18 was rainy but we became the bunk with the most bunk stars. On Days 19 and 20, I got sick. Day 19, we saw *Lord Of the Rings*, the show. It was bad. Day 20 was Alec's birthday and we also saw *Finding Nemo*, the show. Much better. Day 21 was our only normal Monday. We went in the pool, I think (for some odd reason, the dates are screwed up).

On Day 22, Jaron had left B12 and went to B13. We also saw the rest of *50 First Dates*. On Day 23 or 24, we went to an arcade. We were supposed to go to a water park but since it was raining, we went to the arcade. I was doing fine with all my coins.

There was this one game where you pound your fist against this thing and the ball would go through a point value. I got the ball into the 500 spot (I didn't notice) and all of a sudden, these tickets start coming out like two rabbits multiplying! I was concerned. I told Keyoshi that I thought the machine was broken. He was too focused on another thing so all he said was

"Awesome"

Yeah, that really helped! Ben J. of B13 came up and said something like

"You won the 500 prize".

Slap my face, please. I don't win anything. I never won a contest. There was this thing once when I won a Bibleman video when I was in 2nd grade but that's it (the spirit of God was with me. Bibleman is a Christian kids show!).

The tickets kept coming and when it stopped, I took them. Brandon (of my bunk, B12) saw that I had the tickets and asked if he could help. I said it was ok. After Brandon and I folded up all the tickets, I got them exchanged with these cards that say "75 point value" and stuff like that meaning I could get prizes with these points. I got some Peppermint Patties and later, Kenda helped me spend the rest before we left. On Day 25, we saw the counselor show, *Hairspray*. It was pretty good.

Day 26 was the last full day at camp and basically, we were all tired of each other. We did see *Starsky And Hutch*, which was funny. Then we saw a slideshow in the night and a lighting of these rings. I'll admit it: I cried a little. You can't help it. It's very moving that it'll be a long time until you come back. Day 27 was the last day. I was nervous about leaving. Cooper of B10 happened to come from PA so Jeff asked the counselors if it would be okay if Cooper kept an eye on me. It worked out. I did get to meet Trent's dad and some of my bunkmates' parents. Then when I left, I gave all my counselors a hug and a handshake and left.

While on the road, I listened to Kiss. Cooper asked if he could listen to some on his CD player and I let him. When I saw my mom and my sister, I cried. In the car that is. I'm not a girlie man but it just felt SO WEIRD to hear Rebecca's high pitch voice again (not that I missed it!).

Soon after school started, I wanted to write to all my bunkmates. It took such a long time for them to write. In April, I got a letter from Andrew saying that he wasn't coming back to camp but his mother said he would…in the first session. I later emailed Summit and asked who will be in my bunk. I gave them a list of all of the kids I wanted to be with. Oddly, they said that Kyle, Brandon, and Trent were already in B15, my bunk for 2005. I later found out my counselors. One of them is Kenda's sister, Kalyn. I really hope my second year is great and as good as my first year.

THE END!

7th Grade and the first half of the summer (2004-2005)

When I returned to school in September 2004, I wasn't happy. My classes were different and I knew only a few people. However in my exploratory classes, I became familiar with a group of people. They liked me and wanted to group up with me. By the end of the year, I didn't want it to end. I had great teachers and great friends. This year was much better socially than sixth grade.

As I refused to go back to Great Times Day Camp, my mom had me signed up for the Huntington Learning Center. It was boring as hell. I hated it so much. The people there were really nice but this isn't the way one should spend their summer. Luckily, I got out of it and into a two week movie camp. It was at a school and I made a few friends there. I really got to show off my creativity. I couldn't wait to back to camp.

Back in November, I sent a letter to my former B12 bunkmates. Andrew was the only one to reply back, telling me he was going first session for 2005. I had to wait for second session. I already knew the names of my counselors: Kelvin, Jonathan, and Kalyn. Ironically, Kalyn was the sister of Kenda from last year. The day before camp started for second session, I got to talk to Kalyn. She was familiar with who I was and that her sister was my counselor last year. I was expecting it to be as great as my first year and I had plenty of high hopes. Although this year was really good, the result wasn't anything I pictured it to be...

The Camp: Season 2
By Aaron Conn

I had a great time at Summit Camp in 2004 and I wanted to go back. I already had known that I would be back with four (then later five) of my bunkmates from last year. Little did I know that this year would be one of tension, anger, sliding, and plenty of cheese cake. This is the most shocking of the two seasons and overall, it was too quick. LET'S GO!

It was July 26th, 2005. My mom, my dad's mom, and I were going to the hotel that I went to almost a year ago. First, we had lunch. Then, I had to say goodbye to my mom and dad's mom. I cried but soon enough, I was fine when I was in the van. I watched *Sliders* and then tried to sleep. By 3 PM or 4 PM, I was at Summit Camp. I met Kalyn, one of my three counselors. She is the sister of one of my counselors from last year, Kenda. I also met Jim. He was trying to get used to everything. Then I saw Brandon in person for the first time in many months. He said hello in a deep voice! He helped me carry my things and we went into the cabin. Then I saw Kyle and Trent. Kyle yelled "Aaron!" and everyone else was just…there. I found my bed and said hello to Trent. Then all of a sudden, I was being completely ignored. I was very shocked. Then came in an African American counselor and he said

"I got your e-mail. You said you'd bring movies".

I said "Yeah." He looked through my collection and picked out Queen. Soon after, he told me his name was Kelvin and then shook my hand. I was guessing he was Kelvin since I had gotten an email saying who my counselors were. The last of the three I saw was Jonathan. He was quiet and didn't say anything. I saw on his bed a sticker, which read "Jono" (his nickname). Then I also saw a bed saying "Alec". I was shocked.

When I got the email, he wasn't listed. I thought "He's coming back?" Then, we went to hockey (Alec came during this time). After a sweaty game, we went back to the cabin for our showers. Last year, I didn't take one the first day. Things changed and I took one. I started to get nervous on the way to dinner and told John. I asked if I could sit with him and Kelvin. He said that was fine. I also told them about what I eat. We had Horseshoe time after dinner. I read my Jim Morrison book during this time. The evening activity was Movie Night. We watched *The Spongebob Squarepants Movie*. Then it was time for bed. On the way getting dressed I heard Kelvin tell John

"So Brandon is moving to BST2 tomorrow" I ignored it.

I woke up early on Day 2. I noticed there was another counselor in the cabin. It said on his bed "Brian". We had breakfast and then we had chores. We did a few things but then during AI (Athletic Instruction), too many things were on my mind. Brandon leaving, swimming tests, new kid. Yes, a new kid. His name was Jimmy. None of us were prepared for the ride he'd take us on for the whole second session. Anyways, I asked Kalyn if I could talk to her (this was during AI). Then there, I started to cry. It was too much for me.

The swimming tests were fine. We had our weekly picnic lunch, which is good because you don't have to go to the Dining Hall. Then after rest hour, we got a shocking announcement from Kalyn: Periods 5, 6, and 7 were all canceled. That's because it was going to rain. Brian put on a movie from his laptop (Kalyn told me about over the phone). The movie was the first Indiana Jones. I thought I'd like it. Then during the movie, I'm thinking "What the heck is this thing about?" Yeah, I see John Rhyes Davies and Harrison Ford but what is the movie about?!

Anyways, we found that we would waiter like last year. We had early showers. The waiter experience was fine. The evening activity was clubs. Trent and I went to computers.

After clubs, Brandon came up to me and told me that he told a counselor that I had a DVD player. The counselor (let's call her Jessica) wanted to use it during her time On Duty. I talked to Kalyn and told her to tell Jessica no. Next, our counselors told us we would be watching a movie. Our response was "What movie?" We later found out that movie would be *Short Circuit*. It was an old 1986 movie about a robot that had human-like traits.

During the movie, I told either Kalyn or John that Jessica could have my DVD player along with my DVDs. Wrong move. I spent, literally, until midnight trying to get my DVD player back. Where were my counselors? I didn't know. Isn't someone supposed to be on the porch? I went walking to every cabin and tried to talk to anyone. While walking, I found my *Sliders: Season Three* DVD set and took it. By the end of the night, counselors from B12 (how ironic) said that they'd talk to Kelvin.

Day 3 was a pretty good day. I got my DVD player and DVDs back but the sad news was that Brandon was leaving us. I was really upset, though I didn't cry. I just thought "I can still have a good year". Today was trip day and we were going to the movies to see…*The Adventures Of Sharkboy and Lavagirl In 3D*. We were just shocked. How can you take us to see some movie like that? So, Trent and I were together during the movie and it took a while for us to pick a seat. He said he didn't want to be with any other kids. The movie, like I predicted, was a stinker. On a happier note, it was Splash Night. The pool was warm and it was nice.

Day 4 was both a hard and good day. The day began with canoeing on the Delaware River. Then all hell broke loose during Rest Hour when something happened. This thing that happened sent TJ walking off. I couldn't believe it. This was like woman drama. You just don't walk off and then walk around the camp by yourself.

That night was also International Night. Counselors would go up and pretty much explain what it's like in their country. Day 5 was another hard day. During the game night (night, we were playing Snatch the Flag), I talked to John outside about the tensions in the cabin and how I felt. I later went into the cabin and talked to Kelvin. Right there, I cried. I told Kelvin what I told John. I forget what he said but for the rest of the night, I was fine.

Day 6 was a good day but from there on, the year went pretty fast. Jim simply asked if he could watch the first episode of *Sliders*. I said he could and that I'd watch it with him. John watched too and later, Trent came over. For the rest of the year, Jim, Trent, and I remained a "power trio" with *Sliders*.

After dinner it was pouring outside. We stayed in the cabin for the rest of the night. I watched another episode of *Sliders* with John, Trent, and Jim (I only showed them my favorite episodes because we couldn't watch all the three seasons I had within 21 days). Also on this day, we tried to watch the rest of *Short Circuit* but something went wrong with the disc, and we watched *Short Circuit 2*. On Day 7, we had some poor bunk stars (the new system was to have 4 stars for each period. If you had perfect bunk stars, Tim would announce it) but we did have Talent Night.

On Day 8 we went hiking. Unlike last year, we were gone for four periods. On that day, I talked to both John then Kelvin about how I wanted to know the other people in Karli's unit. Kelvin was proud when he heard this and hugged me. Before that, we watched the rest of *Spongebob* and started *Are We There Yet?*, which is one of the worst movies I've ever seen. Day 9 was a simple day. John, Trent, Jim, and I watched two episodes of *Sliders* and I wrote my letters to the other bunks. Day 10 was a pretty good day. We went to Carousel Park. My group was Kalyn, Trent, and Alec. We also had Splash night.

Day 11 was going really well for us. We had perfect bunk stars until in Ropes; we were only given three bunk stars. While on the way to the cabin, there was lots of fighting and all. When we got to the bunk, Karli wanted to see Jimmy, Colin, and I. Karli told us that she had chosen us for Summit's Big Brother Program. I felt honored to have been chosen and accepted it. I just hoped I got a good kid! When I got back to the porch, John had everyone, except Trent and Jim, on the porch. Since there was bad behavior, John decided the order of the showers. So that meant Trent and Jim were in the showers and John said I'd be next. Once John said I could go in, I ran into the cabin away from the tensions outside.

On Day 12, the Big Brother program started and I met Eli. He seemed like a good kid. When I met him, I saw that he was a gamer (he plays Gameboy but he didn't on that day) but I asked him what kind of music he liked. He told me he liked pop and hip-hop music. In a far off galaxy, I heard a record scratch. Then I asked him what his favorite TV shows were. He told me he liked *Kim Possible* and *Kean and Kendelle*. I heard another record scratch. We still did talk about our families.

I forget the evening activity but we did watch *Batman Begins* on Brian's computer. I couldn't understand this piece of crap. Brian obviously must have downloaded the movie from a site. A person must have taped it illegally in a movie theater. When I tried to ask what was happening, Kyle would interrupt me and say "Shut up, Aaron". I put on my DVD player and watched *The Bad News Bears*. Later, I accidentally dropped my DVD player and the movie froze. We went to bed soon after and I went to get changed for bed. Kelvin got a little angry.

Once I was changed, I just couldn't handle myself. I was holding back so many tears and went outside and cried. A counselor was there and he talked to me. I tried my best to tell him what had happened.

Track and Field Day was alright on Day 13. I was very nervous about running. Last year, I didn't and thank goodness because I twisted my muscle in my ankle. This year, there was no pain. From what I see, I was doing good running. I think I ran really well. I think that's because I was put with the kids that run like me. Last year, my bunk was on the Red team and White had won. This year, my bunk was on the White team and the Red team won. Oh well! The next day, I can't remember well. I do know that it was raining and that I was supposed to see Eli. Trent came along with me. After Horseshoe was over, I asked Trent what he thought of Eli. He said he didn't like him and that he could tell he didn't like me. Oh well. That's his opinion.

On Day 15, we had movie night. During this time Trent, Jim, and I watched an episode of *Sliders*. Maria of Yoga had her birthday and we had some cake. During the night, Kyle was bothering me to give him my headphones. I said no but then he went on to say that his mom had died and a message was hidden on a tape (book on tape to be exact, *Eragon*). So I go outside and tell John or Kelvin.

Day 16 I don't remember much though Trent got his DVD player sent and *Sliders* was off the agenda. Jimmy also had a fit over a Too-Too (it's an ice cream sandwich with sugar cookies and it the center is vanilla ice cream, sprinkled with chocolate chips). On Day 17, we went to the Wayne County Fair. I was with Jim and Brian. The next day would have an effect on all of us.

On Day 18, we woke up like every other day. All of us were trying to find our items such as brushes, soap, mirrors, etc. Then we found out. Yesterday while we were at dinner, Alec was back at the cabin going wild. He had taken a bucket, filled it with water and poured it on Brian. This also destroyed our shower wheel (from then on, the counselor would pick the order) and the mirror was tossed out of the bathroom window and was destroyed (from now on, I'd have to use a window outside as my mirror).

I couldn't find my comb. I asked Alec if he knew where it was. He said he threw it out the window, along with other supplies that belonged to us. We were all pissed at Alec. He was very homesick and that may've caused his actions. John later checked in the back of the cabin and found nothing (he was right. Days later, I found my comb). Either way, Alec's parents came over to the camp and Alec went home. It was a pleasant shocker for many of us. I can recall Trent crying because he had lost almost everything. Later that day, the BST/GST's did their two part play of *Star Wars*. It was awful.

On Day 19, my DVD player's screen went bad but before its demise, Trent, Jim, John, and I watched the *Sliders* episode, "The Breeder". We also saw the second half of the *Star Wars* play, which was much better than last night's disaster. The ending was cheesy and too happy but it was fine. Day 20 saw us trying out something I invented called "Bunkvivor". Like Survivor was seven of us were surviving seven periods. Each period (for that day, me) a counselor would pick which of the kids was the worst. By the last period, there would be two finalists. Here's how it worked out:

1st: Jimmy (never came to period)
2nd: Kyle (I think it was him, bad)
3rd: Colin (silly,
4th: Jim (a tie breaker picked a piece of paper and one said "Game Over")
5th: Me (Rock-Paper-Scissors with TJ, best out of 2)
6th and 7th: Trent (3) TJ (2)

TRENT WINS!!!

We never did it again. On Day 21, we had our *Batman Begins* play, which went well. I did the dances. I'm so brave! I also got a voice postcard from my uncle. On Day 22, the last of the two plays, *Westerly Ways* and *SpongeBob*, were performed. I also found both of the *Star Wars* scripts during a game of dodge ball at AI (in the stage room since it was raining).

On Day 23, we had perfect bunk stars and had clubs. There wasn't any computers so Trent and I went to Arts and Craft. I made

B15 stick figures (Kelvin said he looked Japanese on his!). On Day 24, we went bowling. We were supposed to have our Splash Night but Pete's Unit took the pool and we had Robin's Rotation (?), which is a mini version of Track and Field Day.

Day 25 was the day we saw the staff play, *Mamma Mia!* I could tell the plot was changed but it was alright. Trent got a CD case for being at Summit for three years but gave it to me since he had no CDs! Day 26 was an emotional night. However, I had a tape recorder and recorded a hilarious tape. We watched the slideshow, which I was in three times. Then during bedtime, I wanted everyone to watch a Monty Python video I had. However, all the TVs were used and we watched *Teen Wolf* on Brian's computer. Day 27 was the last day. It was so sad to say goodbye. I went on a bus with Kyle and my swimming instructor, Lauren. I cried my eyes out when I saw my mom and my sister. It was good to be home.

During 2005, I didn't keep in contact with any of my former bunkmates until September, I called and IMed Trent. It was really nice talking with him. Will I go back for a third year? Yeah, I will but there's a twist:

I'm Staying For 8 Weeks!

It's scary. It'll be cool to be one of the originals. My only concern is who I will be with. In March of 2006, I emailed Regina, who works at Summit. I explained my concerns for a good bunk and a wanting for me to be with Trent. I haven't gotten anything back yet but I pray to God I do soon. Season 3 will hopefully be better than Season 2 but now I'll be in the STs. I'm a super teen!!!! My worries for Season 3 will still be there until I get that reply from Regina.

THE END!

8th grade (2005-2006)

I'm not going to lie: 8th grade was stressful. It was my last year in middle school. I hate change so this made the year very hard. Like 7th grade, the teachers were very nice although some were a bit intimidating. I stayed after almost every day because I just wanted to get over with my work. I avoided any open-houses for high schools.

Like some students, I was offered to go to a different school that prepared you for your career in the future. My mom and I visited the place and we didn't like it. Still, I avoided anything related to high school because I was anxious. As for socializing, there was some of it. It wasn't like last year where I knew a certain group of kids but it was alright.

I thought about camp sometimes. I did worry that my third year would be worse than my second year. The way I see it, I was expecting too much on every year after my first to be as good as my first. No matter what, my first year is always my favorite. Still, I was worried about staying full session as I had never done it before.

After I spoke with Regina (who organizes the bunks) and sent a few letters, things were looking good. In fact my unit leader, Neale, left a message on my answering machine and said he enjoyed my emails. He said that he was looking forward to meeting me. Right there in the message, he told me the name of my counselors: Carl, Tsur, and Alex.

The day before camp began, I got to speak with Neale on the phone. He told me he would be at the buses when I came. When I told Neale I may get anxious, he chuckled and said I would be fine. I was worried but I still couldn't wait...

32

The Camp: Season 3
By Aaron Conn

Although I had a great time at Summit Camp in 2005, I was still disappointed. I was concerned for my 3rd year. I wrote a letter or two before the year started. I had a reason to be nervous, Compared to my first two years, this would be my first time being at camp for full session. This was my 2nd favorite year. There were more tensions, funny moments, a perfect bunk, and plenty more cheesecake![1] Also, the end of this year would leave an impact on me and still upsets me to this very minute[2]. It would be one of the worst things I ever went through in my life. The ending is so shocking that it even surprised me. However, I did make new friends and have new stories to tell. This is my 3rd year of camp!

It was June 29th, 2006. I was going to the same hotel I went to back in 2004 and 2005. This time, I would be out of my world and in camp for 8 weeks. I was anxious. My mom and my grandma were there with me. I was waiting in a room with many other kids. One of them happened to be Kyle. I said hello to Kyle and we talked for a while. I saw someone else there who would also be my bunk, ST6. His name was Patrick. My mom talked to some from the waterfront. Her name was Amy and she now knew of my anxiety. I didn't cry. I put on my headphones and listened to some stuff.

---

[1] The whole cheesecake gag was the influence Monty Python had on me. It makes no sense at all. I thought it was funny then. I do love Monty Python still!

[2] Just a reminder: This was written around March 2007. I still hadn't got over this certain thing. At the time this book was first published and even before then, I had gotten over it. I don't find it so shocking now but please continue reading!

When we got to the camp, it was strange. I hadn't seen all these things in almost a year! I met my unit leader, Neale. I talked to him the night before camp started. I saw him and one of my counselors, Tsur (pronounced Sir). He also goes by Big T! Tsur was impressed by my heavy bag, which had my CD cases. Tsur took us to the bunk and there were my other two counselors. They were Carl and Alexandra. I said hello to them and went inside the cabin. I had all my things on the bed. From what I remember, it was Carl who came to me and said

"I read your letter. You can talk to us anytime".

I felt better. Then, Alex asked me if I wanted a cup of water and sit on the porch with her. I did and we talked. I did really like Alex. I did get to know her the most out of my three counselors on that first day. Alex and anyone who came into the cabin were impressed by my collection of music. I basically just put all my stuff in my cubby. Everyone else (which included old faces Kyle and Colin, and new faces Brandon, Mark, Nolan, Mitch, and Zeke) was playing PSP's, Gameboy's, DS's, and trading card games. The only kids who weren't doing this were Patrick and another new face, Max. I knew that my friend, Trent, would be coming in July. I had to make a new friend before he came. I thought that I could be friendly with Max.

Soon, we all went to dinner. It felt so weird seeing everyone again. I did get anxious and talked to Carl. We went outside and I cried a bit. I really had to let it all out. We talked for a while. The evening activity was a social for the ST bunks and GST bunks. I wasn't really thrilled by the social. It was like a Horseshoe II. It was basically music, kosher food, kosher drinks, and making out. No thank you! I felt like I had a great first day and I couldn't wait until tomorrow.

The next day, Day 2, I talked to Neale. Alex had taken my digital voice recorder, with permission, from me. I wasn't allowed to have it at all times because it would be illegal to record anyone at the camp and I'd be in trouble. However, I would be able to use it on special occasions.

Neale did tell me some good things that day. He told me I would be serving the medical staff table every time we waitered. When you waiter at Summit Camp, you leave your activity early and go to the dinning hall. You then have to set up the tables and then eat first. After you eat, you get on your waiting gear and get ready for chaos! Since I wrote many letters to the camp and Neale must've read one of them, he gave me the honor of serving that table. I just had to do the opposite, meaning I would serve first then eat with the staff. There was a second waiter when I was eating and his name was Aaron too!

Socially on that day, I did get to talk to Brandon. We talked about the SNL skit, Sprockets. I did get to know a little more about Max. He does like AC/DC! The evening activity was a guy who could balance a Brandonch on his face. Also when I was writing, Zeke and Nolan were bothering me. For all of the first session, they would be the trouble makers of our bunk.

On Day 3, Carl had his day off. Still, we did great. We did meet a helper to the unit. It was an African American counselor named Charlotte, a first year counselor. She would become an important part to this season. I did state in my journal that the issue with Zeke, Nolan, and I was over since Tsur and Alex talked to them. Man, was I so wrong!

We had a social since it was the regular night for one. I did get to find out more of Max's music. He did let me look at his iPod. I scrolled through the artists and found lots of my favorite bands including The Rolling Stones, Aerosmith, AC/DC, and Kiss. I was amazed. However, he had "Greatest Hits" albums by all those bands only which bothered me a tiny bit. I didn't care. I knew that we would get along.

After the social, Kyle did something to me. He kicked me in the crotch. He did kick really hard. I was fine…just then! Day 4 from what I remember was a pretty competitive day. I had my swim test for 25 laps and passed. That was a first for me. We also went out for pizza. It wasn't a trip day. STs have bigger trips and bigger events. So, I ate three slices and really got to have social time with Max. He asked if he could listen to my Ipod. I felt great to have a new friend. The only thing was that Zeke and Nolan were friendly with Max too and treated me like shit.

Day 5 was the 35th anniversary of Jim Morrison's death. I told Alex about this on Day 1 and she kept saying I was a superstar. I had the privilege to have some Doors songs played on the way to 4th period. Zeke and Nolan were still bothering me. It was night was movie night. The movies were *Shark Tale* and *The Day After Tomorrow*. I just listened to the Doors and read.

Day 6 was the 4th of July. I didn't really write about that day but I did write about an incident that happened. When we were walking back from evening activity, Patrick came in last. Now, Patrick does have trouble getting into a conversation and doesn't give the best responses to questions. The bunk called him Patar, which he hated (Note that in an episode of *Spongebob*, there's an episode that takes place before Spongebob was born. The character of Patrick Star had an ancestor called Patar. That's where they got it from).

So when he came in that night, Zeke and his disciples scared him and he screamed. I remember being in the bathroom when it happened but I wanted to run out and help him. Our counselors gave all of us ten minutes off of trip day, which was tomorrow. I didn't like this. I tried to explain that I had nothing to do with it and that I really wanted to help Patrick. Neale and Alex did talk to me but I felt I was still going to get the ten minutes off. Ten minutes was nothing. We were going to Walmart first then a mall.

36

The next day we went on our trip. All four of the ST units came. Our trip days are all day since STs help other counselors during the day. When we got to Walmart, Brandon and I were not going for the ten minutes. I was shocked. My group was Alex, Max, and Mark. I didn't get anything at Walmart but when we got to the mall, it was great. I got two Alice Cooper albums (*Killers* and *Goes to Hell*) and we all got to see a movie of our choice. Max and I saw *Superman Returns* which was alright. I did get to call my mom with my phone card.

On Day 8, Charlotte was back again. I went in a paddle boat with her and she told me that she liked my article (I had done an article on the rock band, Badfinger, which I did in school. I interviewed the keyboardist, Bob Jackson, and had an interview attached. Bob actually emailed me during camp too!). We also had clubs.

During bedtime, Zeke and Nolan were talking from their bed (Zeke and I shared a bunk bed). Zeke went on about the times he masturbated. The conversation got into other nasty things. I told Carl and he said he would do something about it. I didn't like Zeke at all. He and Nolan would continually repeat my name over and over again. For the entire first session, ST6 was the loudest bunk at night.

Day 9 was good. Alex watched my T.Rex DVD thanks to Mitchhew, who kindly lets his bunkmates use his DVD player. She knew almost every song. General Swim wasn't so great. I asked Max early on that if he wanted to come with me and Alex on a paddle boat. He told me he would but changed his mind when Zeke and Nolan told him to go on a kayak. I didn't like that at all.

I took notes down for the camp newspaper for the evening activity which was "A Girl in Love" night or something. Nolan said was trust worthy at bedtime and I made everyone laugh to my Yoda impression. I did my Yoda impression last year and it was funny. I did it again!

Still that night, Kyle came out when I had my time outside (I was allowed to have time outside after the lights went out. This would end soon and I if I wanted to talk to any of my counselors, it would have to be before we went to bed.). Kyle told Carl that Zeke and Nolan were calling him and "chode boy". Chode, apparently, means small penis. I wanted to smack Zeke so badly.

On Day 10, we went canoeing. I was with a counselor named Frasier, Max, and Brandon. On that day we got perfect bunk stars for the first time. However, Carl wasn't with us but he was proud. We had a social that night and when we got back to the cabin, there were only seven of us. Zeke, Mitch, and Brandon (who came shortly after I started to write) were talking to Regina. They were in trouble.

Day 11 was pretty good but the night was bad for me. For sometime, I had a pain in the middle of my legs. I didn't know why. Then I knew why. It was from Kyle's kick on Day 3. I wanted Carl to take me to see Dr. Steve but Tsur took me. Tsur and I really had to hurry. We were going bowling that night.

Dr. Steve had a look at me during horseshoe. He said that I would need to put a heat pad near my areas and see if it felt better by Wednesday or Thursday. If it didn't, I think I heard him say he get someone to "take the blood out". I was frickin' scared when I heard that! Tsur and I ran to the buses but it was too late. They had left us.

Tsur talked to Julie of SIT (who we had for Tribes and would become an important part in the second session) and Julie was unable to get us on a bus. So, Tsur and I got the heating pad and he said that I can sit in the cabin and he would tell me when I should take it off. So, we did that. I did watch a DVD on Mitch's DVD player since Tsur said I could. Neale came by and heard what happened. He saved me a slice of pizza since he was with the pizza group. Isn't that special?! I talked to Carl when he got back. According to him, it wasn't a very good night at the bowling alley.

38

Day 12 was pretty good. I did get to talk to Zeke socially, which was very rare. There was also a movie night. The movies were *The Incredibles* and *X Men 2*.

Day 13 was a quiz night. I got a portable Othello from my mom too in the mail. Also, Tsur told me at boating that Syd Barrett has died. Syd Barrett was from Pink Floyd (I would later find out on Day 15 he died of diabetes.). On Day 14, we went to a different mall and then a theater (last time, the theater was in the mall). I was still with Max and Mark but Tsur was the counselor. I got Alice Cooper's *Constrictor* album and a used copy of *The Crow: Wicked Prayer*. The movie Max and I saw was *Pirates of the Caribbean: Dead Man's Chest*. It was great.

On Day 15, I was disappointed in my bunk. I didn't say why but I think it was because we were pathetic, always in trouble, and didn't have enough cheese cake. I did finish my T.Rex PowerPoint slideshow, which I do not have.

On Day 16, I played Othello with Mitch and then Carl. There was also a Camper Counselor Night, which was alright. Afterwards, we got back to the cabin and Neale came by. He said that he gave one of us the Unit Leader Award. To win it, you had to be mature and great in things. Neale said that the winner was me! As a reward, everyone in my bunk got canteen treats. It felt good but Zeke and Nolan were saying

"Aaron, keep it up and we'll get more of this".

To me, it didn't sound right. I asked Alex that the next time I get a reward like that; I want to be for me only. I wasn't being selfish. It wasn't fair that kids like Zeke and Nolan would get this. "Keep it up" meant I do well, they treat me like shit, and boom! That's not right. I think it was on Night 16 that Zeke talked about the times he had sex. He admits he had it four times and said the second time was the best. Oh, and he keeps condoms in his wallet. Pathetic right? I think this was Day 16 but I know that Alex was on the porch of Night 16.[3]

From what I remember on Day 17, we were having a normal day and I recall that I took a nap during rest hour (which isn't an hour!). I wasn't completely asleep but when I was done resting, it was raining very hard. Jamie of Ropes was watching us and he knew me from nights before when he was OD. We were going to have Adventure World next, which was the ropes course for 3 periods. It was still on except a few of us would go on a biking trip and the rest would stay at camp. Max, Mitchhew, Patrick, Tsur, and I stayed along with some kids and Christine of ST7 (or as we all called her, Mama C). Tsur and Mitchhew weren't there since Mitchhew was having one of his troubles again. I did write that I was upset after the social.

Day 18 wasn't much. We did go out for pizza and something happened during health and fitness. I was trying to get water out of my ear after playing a game and Zeke asked what I was doing. I told him and then he said it made me look retarded. I wanted to smack him. Day 19 wasn't much either. We made t-shirts and had movie night. The movies were *King Kong* and *Ice Age*. I didn't watch either so I got bored and PIMed (Paper Instant Messaging) Carl and Alex. I still have the transcript and I laugh every time I read it.

I would be laughing more on Day 20 when the bunk was introduced to Carl and Alex's personas. When we were waking up in the morning, Carl and Alex weren't themselves. They were two English people named Charles and Polly. I can't remember what they said but I do have a recording from the last full day of camp where I interview Carl as Charles. I talked to Dave of SIT that day

---

[3] She was there on duty for Day 16. I can remember how uncomfortable I felt going to talk to Alex about it. Usually, you wouldn't talk about something like this with a female. You'd ask/tell a guy. I remember Alex and the other person on duty were having fun with it, which is nice!

too about my growing anxiety on high school.

Day 21 was our trip day. We were going to Hershey Park. Many of the kids were excited but I'm not a ride person. We went on an Avery Coach Bus and went to Hershey Park. I was with Max and Charlotte. We still had fun. Chocolate World was the big highlight of the entire trip where everyone could get wasted. There was a tour I went a twice. It wasn't very good but I had nothing else to do but go with Max once and then Alex.

On Day 22, I stated in my journal I was pissed. Zeke and Nolan were on my last nerves. I couldn't wait to see them go. We had a clubs that night and I wanted to go to computers. Since your bunk was showing no respect, we couldn't go.

On Day 23, I read more of my Marc Bolan book. Charles and Polly were back too. We were all nervous to know if Tsur was leaving us. Tsur is in the army and it was undecided if they would need him. Tsur got a text message and it said he was staying with us!

Day 24 was intense from what I wrote. Zeke and Brandon had a fight of which I do not recall. I think it was intense due to the fact it was the end of the first session. Alex, Max, Patrick, Nolan, Kyle, and I all went hiking that day with some ST7 people. We saw a slideshow that I appeared in once (I appeared in a film part). We were all excited about tomorrow. Our parents were coming!

It was Day 25 and our parents came to visit us. My dad's parents, my mom's mom, and my mom all came to see me. It felt weird seeing them again. My dad's parents gave me a DVD I asked for. It was *Harold and Maude*, which I wanted to see again.

There were several options. We could go to a carnival type thing, eat, or walk around the camp. I showed my family the camp and saw some familiar faces. My dad's parents left early and my grandma and mom stayed for a while longer. When they left, I started to cry but I tried to hold back my tears. When I went into the cabin and saw Alex, she came up to hug me once I started to cry.

Good news was that Nolan was out. There were nine of us left now. We had our normal dinner and then went out bowling. Mitch was nice enough to lend me his DVD player so Max and I could watch *Harold and Maude*. We didn't finish it but I watched all of it and then showed Max the rest on Day 26. He didn't really like it but hey. In the morning of Day 26, Zeke left so he could go on a plane back home. I was jumping with joy. That bastard was out of the damn bunk! Mark left later on and then there were seven of us left. We had lots of periods off. I showed Max *Sliders* and he thought it was good. We easily had perfect bunk stars that day!

By the end of the Day 26, I was excited for Session 2's start. Trent and a kid named Elliot were joining us. I knew this was going to be loads of fun. Max, Trent and I would be a power trio. I could just feel it. I was right but the end of my third year is so shocking, it still upsets me to this very minute. It would change my relationships and have a huge impact on me.

This ends Session 1 and below is Session 2. Take a break, do jumping jacks, or push ups. Get ready for Session 2!

On Day 27, we woke up to find there was still seven of us. Trent and Elliot were coming alright but we had one more counselor coming. It was Paul from the Waterfront. He would stay in our cabin for the entire session. Paul is English and has long curly hair. Soon after lunch, we were in the bunk. I wanted to see Trent so badly. Then he came. I went down with Carl to see Trent and greet him. Trent would sleep above me, where Zeke used to sleep. His parents kind of said hello to me but they left soon and then Elliot came soon after. He seemed like a nice kid and he is.

During Karate, I decided to sit out with Trent. Although there was a no talking rule, I couldn't help but chat up with Trent. We

42

talked about what was going on in our lives and other things. It was cool. We also had a trivia night. I also had an attempt to get Trent and Max talking. I think I did the dumbest thing ever just asking them to fill out stuff. Even talking about it makes me embarrassed.

Day 28 was pretty good. We had our trip day and went to the state park and then back to the Steamtown mall. My group was Trent, Max, and Tsur. Trent and I hung out at the park chatting up. I tried to get Max in. It is very hard for a person like me who has trouble making friends to have two at once in the same place. I thought I'd go for the power trio and see if we could bond as three. It happened with Andrew in Season 1 and also with Jim in Season 2. This was the new three. You could call me the leader but that sounds a little too bossy. I just tried to have us close.

I got some things at the Steamtown mall. I got *This Is Spinal Tap* on DVD and several CD's. They were Alice Cooper's *Hey Stoopid*, Pink Floyd's *The Piper at the Gates of Dawn*, and a compilation by T.Rex. Trent and I then went to an arcade place and had some fun.

On Day 29, we got perfect bunk stars. Trent, Max, and I watched This Is Spinal Tap. Paul and I looked at each other's iPods. He had a lot of albums by Pink Floyd and a similar musical taste. During clubs, Colin got mad for some reason. When he was sitting there in line, he hit me with his Magna comic book. It was the spine of the book he hit me with. He apologized but it was pretty freaky.

Day 30 was another day of perfect bunk stars. We had Home Ec. and at night, we watched the international night show. I sat outside and listened to my Pink Floyd album I got from Day 28 (I had listened to my Alice Cooper one the day before with Trent). We also waiter and Trent took the place of the kid that was there first session.

Day 31 was good but the night was terrible for me. First off, we had our third day of perfect bunk stars. So we had a bunk movie. The movie was *Pay It Forward*. Trent asked me if he could watch my *Spinal Tap* DVD and watch the never-before-seen footage. I had to say no because if he was going to watch it, I wanted to watch it also. My mom had viewed it way back in 2003 and said to not watch that footage. Trent got a bit angry and I went outside.

I think my behavior that night was a bit over-the-top. I was crying over this whole thing[4]. I wrote on a piece of paper of how I was feeling. I think it was because of my strong writing skills, they said to do this from now on.

Day 32 was fun. We had our fourth day of perfect bunk stars. We went out for pizza and I sat at a table with Trent, Max, and Elliot. However during Health & Fitness, we were playing Drip, Drip, Drop. I sat out because I didn't want to get wet. Colin comes over and says,

"Drop!"

I was both pissed and upset that he got me wet. I think my reaction was a little over-the-top again! Day 33 was good also. We had our 5th day of perfect stars. Trent and I watched the first two *Planet of the Apes* films. Max joined us at times and apologized that he wasn't watching much. We told him he could join us anytime. I think that was the wrong thing to do. I should've really done what Max wanted to do. Anyways, there was a movie night and they watched *Spider-Man 2*.

I didn't write much for Day 34. We did have Karaoke night. I told Kyle to pick "Girls, Girls, Girls" by Motley Crue because it would be funny. Instead Patrick, Kyle, and I went up for "The Long

---

[4] Okay, something was unclear here. The reason why I didn't want to watch *Pay It Forward* was because my mom and her boyfriend had seen the movie. My mom told me about it and spoiled the ending (I won't spoil it here but the ending is not happy at all!).

and Winding Road". I didn't sing. I just sat up there and helped them. Honestly, I felt like grabbing the microphone because I have a decent voice! We also had our sixth day of bunk stars in a row. Trent and I watched the third *Planet of the Apes* movie and bits of the fourth.

Day 35 was a trip day. We went back to the state park and went in the pool there. Then we went to the movies. Trent, Max, Alex, and I went to see *Cars*. It was my second time seeing it. Then we went to Honesdale park and had pizza and soda.

Day 36 was another day of perfect bunk stars. Trent and I saw the rest of the fourth *Planet of the Apes* film and some of the fifth. As a reward for having seven perfect days of bunk stars, we had hamburgers that Neale and Tsur went out to get. I don't like hamburgers so I didn't have anything but I'm not sure if I got anything in exchange.

Day 37 was the day of Brandon. I learned four things from him that day. I'm a jackass, a rat, I suck, and I'm going down. He did get pissed in the morning when I was sweeping and some of his Yu-Gi-Oh card went in the trash. I feel sorry but he can't have them on the floor. He also drummed at the second Camper Counselor night. I didn't clap. The second CC night wasn't very good. I thought the one from Session One was a bit better.

Trent and I finished the *Apes* saga and started *The Crow*. We also had our eighth day of perfect bunk stars. Day 38 was our ninth day of perfect bunk stars. We went canoeing on the Delaware. I was in a canoe with Alex and Trent. I was acting up! Trent and I also finished up *The Crow* and watched the second. I let him finish the second one up at night.

Day 39 was our tenth perfect day of bunk stars. Brandon called Trent and me gay. We joked about it and said we sure were! Besides watching the third *Crow* film, we went to Walmart. I got

45

Pink Floyd's *Meddle*. Trent had $45 and spent it on water, claiming this was *real* water. I was jealous of his wealth and he got pissed. It just got me wondering.

On Day 40, it was official. Our record of perfect bunk stars was over after Video and Radio. My word of "Bunkvivor" inspired Carl and Alex to set up a reward game. We didn't vote off but we had to get points and pick a prize or something. Later on, the whole thing was dismissed.

Day 41 was Track and Field day. We were the Red team. Colin kept saying that day that the scores were fixed and it was all faked. Red came in second that day but we did great. On the Rec Hall field, people were amazed at our teamwork. Trent and I were good. I guess I said that in my journal because we did have some disagreements. The next day was one of my worst days of camp ever and it would change my friendship with Trent.

On that trip day of Day 42, we were going to the Wayne County Fair. The group was Max, Mitchhew, and Tsur. We didn't go on any ride but still had some fun. When I was at the Fair, I started to worry about the end of the year. I would be in high school in only a few weeks. There was a so called secret place after the Fair I heard. We were going to the Old Country Buffet.

Since I hadn't been with him all day, I wanted know if Trent wanted to sit with me at the OCB. I got up to him and asked. Shockingly, he said

"Get away from me."

Confused, I tried asking him again. He said that he was tired of me and I was like a cat. I felt like crying. What did I do wrong? Anxious, I sat in the back with Tsur and told him what happened. He said he would talk and settle down once we get back from camp. I agreed and tried to relax. The OBC was great. I didn't sit with Trent and sat with Tsur and Max since there wasn't any room left at the table where the other ST6 people were sitting.

On the ride back, everybody was wasted on ice cream. I know it sounds weird but I think it was the caffeine from the chocolate ice cream or the sugar that made them all wound up, including the counselors. When we did go back to camp, I asked Carl if I could talk to him privately and brought Trent. I told Carl the situation. Trent said he has been tired with my music, stories, and all that he hasn't been interested in.

I was a bit shocked because he was showing interest whenever played music for him and the bunk. He said he just wanted his space. It sounded easy enough but once he left, I cried my eyes out. Carl and I talked a bit longer. I then went into the bunk and just told myself to forget and tomorrow will be better. I wrote in my journal in the bathroom stall alone. It's pretty much how I felt and I still feel this right this minute[5].

On Day 43, I woke up and just couldn't stop thinking about the day before. From the beginning of the day to Period 6, Trent and I didn't talk. During Period 6 at woodshop, I did speak with Trent with Tsur helping. Tsur mentioned to spend more time with Max, who I totally forgot about. I did hang out with Max more until the end of the year. I cried during swimming instruction and Tsur said he'd talk to Trent. However at night, we didn't have an evening activity. It was for the *Narnia* play we were doing so Trent and I played some games.

However on Day 44, Trent told me he wanted his space for the entire day. I was a bit shocked but it was just too much pressure. During Home Ec, I cried again. We were going to have an early lunch since we were going to have a general swim during rest hour, which is so stupid. I was so upset outside. I remember that Trent

---

[5] Another reminder: I'm over this now. Okay?

came out and I said,

"You mentioned about the friendship ending"

That must've been the dumbest thing I ever said. Trent then responded by saying it could be. Three seconds later, he said,

"You know what? It's over. Bye."

Now even more upset, I didn't know what to do. When we were ready to go for general swim after lunch, I spoke to Trent once again. Of course, my speech failed and I went into the cabin. When Carl and Tsur asked me to come out, I just couldn't. So, they left me there in the cabin alone. I still don't know if they were angry or they thought I just needed some time to relax. Thinking I shouldn't be in the cabin alone, I tried to get myself relaxed and headed down to the lake.

While walking, I saw Alex. We sat down in the Rec Hall field and talked. I told her what had happened because I think she didn't quite know what the thing between Trent and I was (she had a day off on Day 43). She told me I had to have a positive attitude and then proceeded to get Justin from woodshop. I just had to look them in the eye and say,

"I am a positive person."

It was very embarrassing but soon enough, Alex had me said it to Mama C and even Trent. Trent didn't believe it and then he told someone from ST7 that I had something to say to them. Who made Trent in charge? During Discovery, Trent sat out somewhere for poor behavior and started to cry. I was confused but that showed that he was the softest bully I've seen. Wrong. He still said I wasn't his friend. He also said in other periods I was annoying, boring, and that I didn't have any friends.

After my shower, Alex got me to talk to Julie of SIT. I

explained to Julie outside about the situation. I agreed to give Trent his space until rest hour tomorrow and see what happens. That day, we ranked #2 in the chart of perfect stars in the STs. For that, we watched *Finding Nemo*.

On Day 45, I found out Trent hated me. I think it was during lunch he said he didn't like me because of my medication. What the hell was he saying? I spoke to Julie again and the next agreement was to give Trent his space until tomorrow morning (which later was changed to rest hour), where she would talk to both Trent and I.

That night was the *Narnia* play. I didn't want to go onstage and asked to help. After the show, several other kids and I were taken with Charlotte (who was now a counselor for ST4) to the ST4 cabin. I knew why. We didn't go onstage and we wouldn't get any canteen treats. I was pretty pissed because I asked so many times to help. Also, I was hungry since dinner was so bad. I didn't ask earlier and that's why I wasn't with them.

I cried and talked to Alex. She said that I was a lot like her and that we would talk for a period during the day (which never happened). Tsur also spotted a meteor shower and everyone went outside. I was so pissed that I didn't go out.

Day 46 was pretty short. We had some periods off. Julie talked to Trent and I. Trent was so pissed. He just wanted to get the hell out of there. I also called my mom due to the progress of this issue. I hoped she could give me some advice. It was funny because the first few times I kept getting this guy named Tom (or Phil. I can't really remember his name). He was so pissed that Tsur said he threatened to call the police! Tsur even thought about picking up the phone and saying,

"Tom, join the Israeli army."

We had a movie night and it was *Brandonchwarmers*. So, I

hung out with Brandon of Rob's unit and watched *Survivor*! Day 47 was short also. We saw the unit plays of *Back to the Future* and *Beauty and the Beast*. Both were fair attempts. In fact, I used Mitchhew's DVD player and played the first *Back to the Future* movie.

Day 48 was quick. We saw the last unit plays of *Wallace And Gromit* and *The Simpsons*. Both were very bad. I went on a kayak for the first time. It was fun. I did go over to Trent, who was in a canoe. I asked him if he had his space. He pushed the kayak back and said he wanted more space.

We also had a Round Robin. It's kind of like a shorter Track And Field Day. This was the first one for STs, who normally don't have Round Robin. My prediction was we wouldn't win. The prize was an ice cream party the day before we left for home. I was right and Rob's unit won. I was pissed. I just hoped they stuffed themselves sick.

Day 49 was our last trip day. We went to Dorney Park. My group was Mitch, Max, Brandon, and Tsur. We still had some fun and went to the arcade many times. I also got a glitter globe thing for my sister, which broke. Tsur got another for me. How nice is that?

We also saw Nolan! We really did. His family came over and found Summit! We also had a hard time coming back to camp. The traffic was really bad. So, we slept in the next day.

Day 50 was pretty good. I was in computers twice. Also, I started talking to Trent more during swimming instruction (it was free swim and I was fishing for him or something). There was also some Prom thing for the STs. Everyone was trying to dress up and look nice. I called them all womanizers!

The last days were hard. Trent and I were getting along more but I hated his Alex friend from ST7. I found Alex very annoying.

Tsur also helped me pack and Trent helped too. There also the play for *Grease*. Carl had a part in it. It was good. I also got a CD case for being in the camp three years.

Day 52 was our last full day. It was hard. Trent and I watched *Sliders*. It also rained and we only had General Swim. People from ST6 and ST7 watched *Fun with Dick and Jane*. I didn't watch. I also recorded Carl as Charles and Alex as Polly. I still think it's funny. We also had our slideshow. I was in this one three times. Since it was raining, we saw the 2006 sign lighten on the big screen in the Rec Hall. I was very overwhelmed the way back.

Day 53 was a painful day. Trent was starting to have a mean attitude again. I played the recording of Charles and Polly just for laughs. I went on the coach bus with Kyle, Patrick, and Max. Heather from Boats was there too. I started cry when I was in the car with my mom and sister. I was still glad to be home.

I haven't really kept in contact with my bunkmates. I did keep in contact with Carl, Alex, Julie, Max, and Trent. I called Trent two times and he was very rude. I did call Max a few times. In Late April and early May, I found out who would be in my bunk so far. It turns out that Kyle, Max, Brandon, Colin, Nolan, Mark and a new kid named Nick are in my bunk so far. Max is only staying second session though.

As for Trent, he isn't coming back according to Summit. I might call him but I think I'll never see him again. This means that in Season 4, I'm going to make a new friend. I'd like to look at my 3rd in a positive way. There were some crazy moments and some bad moments. Although I have doubts about Season 4, I'm looking forward to it.

THE END!

The Camp: Season 4
By Aaron Conn

You think after the incident I had last year at Summit Camp in 2006, I'd never want to come back again. You're wrong. I wanted to do it again and see what it was like this time around. However, Trent wouldn't be there. I would be forced to make new friends and reconnect with old ones. This year is one of fights, dirty humor, melt downs, and plenty of laughs. Overall, this is the weirdest of all the years. This is my fourth year!

Preface
      Yes, this preface is necessary! If you read about my third year, I was an emotional wreck after that year ended. I felt as if I could never have friends again. Also, I was nervous as hell about beginning high school. Towards the end of my school year, I was doing extremely well. I even got in the *Who's Who of American High School Students*, which is saying a lot. Still, I was very timid and quiet. Explaining the Trent incident was hard because it's such a long story. I did actually call Trent twice after camp had ended and he was very nasty. In May or June, I called him again. He said he wasn't coming back and didn't get angry at me or say anything rude. One other thing that changed was his voice! I ended that call telling I'll miss him and I think we are just 'cool' with one another, which has made me sleep better.

      I also called Max a few times, who said he'll be coming second session. In early June, I wrote my traditional letter to my counselors and unit leader. A week or two later, the phone rang and my mom answered and soon gave the phone to me. It was Neale, my unit leader from last year. He told me things got rearranged for this year and that he was going to be my unit leader again. Not only that but Neale also said I would be with Carl again, one of counselors

52

from last year. He did this to ease my anxiety and Carl called me the next day.

Carl was proud of me and what I had accomplished. He told me the kids who were coming and also my counselors. I would have four instead of the usual three. There was a guy name Chris who would be the person to straighten up the boys in the unit (kind of like what Charlotte from last year did). Chris would be sleeping in our cabin. I would also have TWO girl counselors named Bekka and Sammie-Jo. Also staying was a guy named Simon, a specialist for Discovery. I was excited and ready…

It was June 21st, 2007. The year was starting so early, my last day of school had been the day before! Coming with me was my mom, my dad's mother, and my younger sister. We had lunch at the restaurant there. While eating, I spotted Kyle. He would be with me this year once again.

We all then went to the room where everyone else was. I spotted Patrick, who would be with me again this year. Also in the room was Byron. I remembered his face but didn't know his name. I didn't cry while going on the bus. I wanted to make sure that anyone on the bus (not a van) knew about my anxiety.

Sitting next to me was Kyle. He seemed very friendly and was showing me what he had to keep him occupied. When we got to the camp, it was so weird. One by one, bunks were called out of the bus. Kyle, Patrick, Byron, and I came out for ST11. Neale was there to greet us and so was Bekka.

We went up to the cabin, which used to be a girls cabin according to Neale. There on the porch was Carl, who looked like a mother greeting his grown kids on Christmas day. We all gave hugs and went inside to find our beds. I sat there on my bed for a while, scoping the room. I saw new faces such as Joel, Noah, and Brent. When I read the list of kids early on, pictures of them were coming into my mind. I thought they'd all be a bunch of GameBoy freaks and all. These boys looked like they could kick my ass!

Mark from last year was there too and so was Nolan, who had grown his hair out. He seemed friendly and would be for the rest of his stay. Without Zach, he was a better person. Arriving late was Colin. While we all just sat there, I put on some Thin Lizzy. I played "The Boys Are Back In Town", which Carl pointed out that the boys *are* back in town. Brent then started to notice my music and seemed to have an interest in it. Carl gave me a list of the kids of session one and how long each was staying. Only Byron, Noah, Kyle, and I would be staying the whole time. Julie from SIT came in and said hello to me.

Sammie Jo also introduced herself to me. It seemed very cool and everyone was being so nice after a long, stressful bus ride. Neale came in later and told us that we would be waitering for dinner. I was so anxious and pulled Carl aside and cried. I wouldn't be waiting for the medical staff but instead, for B14. Carl understood and told me he'd be on a "5 minutes cup of water" patrol or something. Mama C, from last year, saw this and smiled.

Colin came in after we were done. Waitering was fine. Also, on that day was Brent's birthday. We all had the cake in the cabin and then had a "walking" horseshoe since it was raining. We then had our first night social. I was quiet and reading a book about Phil Lynott of Thin Lizzy. Joel and Brent seemed to really stick out as friendly and outgoing. After the social, I wasn't feeling good emotionally. I talked to Sammie and really did connect with her. I slept that night with confidence.

Day 2 was alright. We didn't have swimming tests but we did do everything else. Brent was not present for most of the day. He was very homesick and I felt like helping or something. Brent was only staying for first session and that was a shame because I was kind of becoming friendly with him.

I tried to have a conversation with Joel during the rest period. He looked at my collection of 300 plus CDs and didn't really find anything. He did say he liked Black Sabbath, which at the time I only owned two albums by. As of now, I've been buying more Black Sabbath! During Horseshoe, I tried to talk to Noah. I asked him what he had been listening to on his CD player. He said he liked rap and some rock. I thought that was the end but when someone asked him if he was going to the Friday night services, he said

"I can't come. I'm half Christian and half Jewish."

This was not the end of the conversation. I asked him about that and told him I was the same. For those of you who don't know, my mom is Christian and my dad was Jewish. For him, it was the opposite way around. I later talked to Carl about the new kids and he seemed proud. He talked to me in his Charles accent.

If you remember last year, he and Alex were these two English people called Charles and Polly. Alex, sadly, wasn't there that year. I suggested to Carl before about continuing Charles but the story was that Polly sent her sisters Holly (Bekka) and Dolly (Sammie) to teach them how to become ladies. Carl didn't accept it at first but on that day, he did!

Still after talking to him, I wasn't happy. I was jealous of Joel and Brent's magical powers they had to make everyone their friend. I didn't have that power and I was a depressed son of a bitch for the rest of the night. We saw Steve Max again, like last year. He was the guy who could balance a bench on his face. I wrote my journal entry there. I ended it with saying that my goal was to become friends with Joel and Noah.

Day 3 was less tense than the day before. I still had my jealousy but I went through it for the day. It was cold by the end of the day. At biking, Carl let me wear his cheap sweat pants. I don't know what material that thing was made from but I ripped the pants at least three times. Carl was cool with it and he said he'd have them sewn by someone in textiles.

During that period, I asked Neale if I could speak with Julie one of these days because I was so depressed and worried. Neale told me I was nervous all the time! However, he said he would try to arrange it and said that this year should be better without Zach and Matt!

During dinner, I felt a connection with Byron. He was nice to pass me the food I wanted to eat but he was pretty much a trouble maker. Most of the time, the trouble maker doesn't like me. Byron seemed nice to me and I felt good. That night, we had our cheesy job interviews for the ST work program. I picked newspaper, computers, and unit leader assistant. I would later get newspaper and unit leader assistant, since I spoke strongly about them.

While waiting before, I felt so depressed that I blared Thin Lizzy in the cabin. Kyle thought I was an emo and told me to "put on some fucking headphones" I think. This is how I feel, man. Get use to it. Besides, it's better that the shit you listen to. In my journal, I put down that I felt as if I socially gotten along with Joel.

Still, I was upset by the fact that he'd be gone after first session. The night was wild. Everyone was speaking loud and talking dirty. I think it was Sammie who came in and said that we were too loud. This felt bad for Joel and I, who were angels. From what I remember, Kyle got up out of his bed and everyone had a flashlight on him as he masturbated in front of everyone. This, fortunately, lasted for only seconds. Still by the end of the night, I was angry and upset.

Day 4 was pretty good from what I can remember. It was funny that day because I came up with idea that Carl couldn't sing or dance for the day, which he always did. Everyone seemed to like the idea and Carl was tortured for that day! We did activities such as soccer, karate, music, and our swimming tests. Carl helped me out with that because I told him I was very afraid. We also had ceramics, which was funny because the instructor referred to the clay as a rubber kidney. I said that was a great name for an album! For the evening activity, we had a lame *Nacho Libre* movie night.

I talked with Carl once again during this. I told him how I was feeling and about my growing jealousy of not finding a friend. He said everyone in the bunk was my friend. I said no to that. Joel and Brent were not friends yet. This is what I like to call get-alongers[6]. So I said that Joel and Brent were people I just talked to. Carl then said that's what a friend is. Oh really? You mean if I ask some guy who just robbed a 7 Eleven what time it was, he's my friend? He's an idiot from what I know because he's robbing a freaking store!

Anyway, I asked Carl if a kid at camp from first session could also stay for second session too. He said that it has happened once or twice but it's very rare. I told him I wanted Joel to stay. Carl told me not to worry about them leaving and enjoy the time I have with them now. He was right. Still, I asked Joel if he ever considered

---

[6] In the first edition, I also said I call them PITT (People I Talk To). I've never used it. Probably for a very short time but my God, that abbreviation is corny. I think the word I was looking for then and that I use now is "acquaintances".

thinking about staying for the next session. He said his dad (his mother passed away so we got something in common) had him signed up for all these other camps. I told him it's possible. He said he'd have to think about it.

On Day 5, I finally got to talk to Julie. I told her about my concerns and cracked a few jokes here and there. We also had tribes with Julie and during that time, Colin juiced out titles for an idea I had about a concept album. On that day, we had a nature walk and went over to Toby's Rock. Toby's Rock is an icon there. It's said that hundreds of year ago, a guy named Toby came over to Rose Lake and found this rock or something. I'm not completely sure but in my mind, I thought that it would make a killer rock opera!

Colin, who has the some of the same musical tastes as me, helped out by having song titles written out. The only problem was I can't write a song or play an instrument. I did later try to write non-serious songs but the thing remains uncompleted. Maybe next year I'll do something with it! Also that day during dinner, I talked with Joel about him staying longer. He said wants to and asked me if I wanted him to stay. Of course, I wanted him to stay.

During Horseshoe, Noel from Adventure asked me if I'd like some help with my biking. We'd have to set it up tomorrow. I said yes to him. We had clubs that night and still at the end of the night, I was jealous and angry. This time, it was Byron and Joel. Byron was the oldest of the bunk, since he was going into 11th grade. I was under the impression everyone else was going into 10th grade like me but I'll go into that later.

Back at the cabin, I pulled off my acting skills. The scene was a depressed 15-year-old boy who feels lonely. Action! Simon came over and asked what was wrong. I tried to keep it short but I told him to ask Carl about last year's incident. Simon said he would and I slept with some confidence. The next day was so shocking that it needs an intro for itself. Before Day 6, Kyle had been an asshole every day. He would flash us and also be nice at times. I had been depressed since Day 1 and I didn't know why. None of us were ready for tomorrow...

In the morning of Day 6, we all woke up as usual and got dressed. Kyle was in his sleeping bag and flashed us twice. We didn't know why. I thought it was just Kyle being Kyle. Carl also had his day off. For the first few periods, we were a group of nine instead of a group of ten. After fourth period, Chris said Kyle was going home. Everyone was spreading rumors on why and I myself wanted to know.

We had lunch soon after but when we got back, all of Kyle's things were gone. His bed was empty. Neale spoke to us all and said that Kyle was picked up by his grandfather. He was gone for the year. Neale said he was sorry that Kyle didn't come over to say goodbye, which Colin was upset about. Why was he leaving? We were never told although all of us know why. The reason why Kyle was kicked out will remain confidential in this essay. All of us were so happy. I felt odd but after a while, I was so happy he was gone. For the rest of the day, I felt great.

After my shower, I went out on the porch and saw that Joel, Brent, and Noah were all talking. I joined them. It got to the point where Joel asked us if we ever "fucked a girl". Brent said he did and Noah said so too. Joel said he never did. The question then came to me. I said I've never been in a relationship with a girl and I'm struggling to have more friends. So maybe when I'm about 18, I may have one. I'm not sure. To my surprise, they all said it was okay if I didn't have a girlfriend and that made me feel great. I'm kind of against subjects like that but it was directed to me and I told them the truth[7].

However, one of them was lying which I'll get to later. For a reward in the evening (probably for getting perfect stars or something else), Chris set up a TV with a DVD player and some junk food for *our* evening activity. We all voted for our own DVDs. I wanted it to be one of my DVDs but having only very few movies and most of them being "boring" documentaries on music, my movies were just too old for them and they decided to watch *South Park*. I was so pissed. Sammie saw this and we talked. She said to give it a try but I found the show very offensive. Sure, it was censored and all but I hate the show. Tomorrow was trip day so at least there was something to look forward too.

Day 7 was our trip day. However, there was a change this year. Instead of going on trips the entire day, the first four periods would be clubs. We had previously signed up to be in certain groups. We would then have lunch and then go on the buses to our trip. This would not be done for the trips to Hershey Park and Dorney Park. We had a pirate game in our unit (or something). We won first and had canteen treats as the "treasure". I also found out Joel was going into 9th grade. We then had our club activity and I got to go to computers. We then had lunch and then went on the buses.

The trip was to the Steamtown mall and a choice of four movies to see at the theaters across the street. All the movie choices sucked but I decided on *Evan Almighty*, which wasn't that bad. My group for the mall was Sammie, Joel, and Brent. In short, I bought *Over-Nite Sensation* by Frank Zappa, *A Saucerful Of Secrets* by

---

[7] This is making me cringe. I could've worded this better but the thing I was trying to say is that emotionally and socially, I didn't have the capability of having a relationship. At the time I write this, I'm almost 20 years old and I still haven't been in a serious relationship. Don't get me wrong: it would be nice to be in one but I think it's just a matter of how time-consuming it is. Moving on…

Pink Floyd, and a used copy of *Women And Children First* by Van Halen. Everyone else got guy spray or clothes.

Day 8 was a usual day at first. We had the first four periods but then it was raining during rest hour (which is really 45 minutes). We tried to go to a period at first in the rain but then there was thunder and it really started to pour. So, we ran like hell to the cabin and had some laughs. I had brought my digital voice recorder again but Carl accepted to keep it a secret. If it became a problem with everyone else, Carl would take it for a short time. So, I got some funny recordings which include Carl singing "My Favorite Things" and interviewing him as Charles.

We also relied heavily on the Orb. The Orb was like a Magic 8 Ball and it was 90% right all the time. We also relied on it in my third year. They also wanted to ask it dirty questions. For example, Byron asked if he'd ever get a blow job. It said no or something and he said he had one already! Eventually the rain stopped and we went to nature during 7th period. For the evening activity, we had a trivia night and canteen. I also got a 20Q Music from my mom in a package. Bekka wasn't there that day since she lost her voice.

Day 9 was a special day. We got a new guy in the bunk that day. During AI, Neale transferred Brandon from ST10 to ST11. I was excited but if I would do something weird like make a sound, he would give me a "What the fuck man?" kind of look. It would take while for him to adjust to his new bunk but by the end of the session, I'm happy to have known Brandon. Anyways, we got a reward to go to the Nintendo Hut. I wanted out because Byron, as much as I like him, had some really bad music playing. I was also jealous of Brandon's presence at first because I was having a ball without Kyle.

Also, people really wanted to see how "dumb" Patrick was. Patrick is one who can't give the best response to questions and everyone hated him. I defended him last year and this year too. It's not my favorite job but the leave the guy alone! Everything calmed down for me. Neale even hung out in the cabin during showers. We saw a stupid *The King and His Jealous Family* show. Carl and Neale were in it and rocked!

Day 10 was funny and bad towards the end. The funny thing was drama and video & radio. In drama, we came up with the idea to do a play with good guys and bad guys. It was decided the good guys were on the look for something. Being a die-hard Alice Cooper fan, I suggested the thing to be pants![8] We called it *Lord of the Pants*.

It starts off with Borat (Joel) and Shaggy (Brent) explaining that the world is held together by four pairs of pants. They come to a tree house where Yoda (me. From what I'm told, I have an excellent Yoda impersonation) while Cruela Devile (Carl) is listening in. We battle her and Emperor Palpatine (Nolan) and finally Patrick.

The bad part was the social. Sammie and Chris put this hair gel so I look nice and all for, I don't know someone of the opposite sex. They failed as I read my Phil Lynott book. This also got me upset with Joel and Brent again. I talked to Simon about this and I forget what he said. I know it was just a joke but if now when someone makes fun of me or makes a comment about me dating, I won't be happy. However, we had our first day of perfect bunk stars.

---

[8] I know some people don't get this. Alice Cooper has had a syndicated radio show since 2004. When he asks a trivia question and someone gets it right, Alice will award that person a pair of pants. Now why pants? According to Alice's autobiography in 2007, he and his daughter Calico (who goes on tour with him) will hit the shopping malls once they arrive at a new venue. It turns out that they buy one too many pairs of pants. Alice will give the pants away to a person who gets a trivia question right. He'll also autograph the pair of pants.

Day 11 was our second day of perfect stars. However, it was chilly throughout the day and only Joel and Brent did their Delaware tests. The rest of Neale's unit came down to the dining hall for games and hot chocolate. We had soccer and a bunk period to watch the *Family Guy* movie about Stewie Griffin's future and all. I had seen it before and thought it was funny but not the greatest thing ever. I did eventually come in and watch some of it. Since then, I've come to accept *Family Guy* and I enjoy watching it now although *The Simpsons* are way better.

I also remember having slow service during dinner. I sat near with Joel and Brent and we were waiting for the peanut butter. Remember that the camp is kosher so the food is really bad most of the time. However, Chris came down towards the end with bowls of peanut butter and jelly! It was so cool for us so we dug in! We had a movie night and watched *Casino Royale*.

Day 12 was pretty interesting. We were working for bunk stars but at second period at woodshop, we were given only two stars. Joel then suggested the idea of earning back the stars. Carl, Bekka, and Sammie liked it and at the end of that day, it was our third day of perfect stars. I also started my newspaper job. To my surprise, the discovery people are in charge of it and Simon happens to be one of them. However, Sam instructed us that day and I found it kind of lame. I liked Sam though!

It was before dinner, I bent over pick up something and I tore a muscle in the lower part of my back. It was hard for me to walk. Brent kindly let me use his DVD player and I watched a Thin Lizzy DVD.

On Day 13 we got our fourth day of perfect stars cheaply, once again. We had Home-Ec. that day but the instructor was sick.

So, Neale asked if any of us would like to come down with him and make something. Cooking with Neale? Sounds like a TV show but yeah I'll do it. Along with me were Joel, Brent, Byron, and Brandon. Mama C dropped by to and Neale taught us how to make egg-in-a-hole. We also had sugar smoothies but it was all hush-hush!

For the evening activity, we had a Field Game Night. I remember getting strict on Brent but that was because of my back, which hurt badly. I also put on *This Is Spinal Tap* during rest hour on Brent's DVD player. No one seemed thrilled. Oh well.

Day 14 was the Fourth of July. We also had a trip day. We would've gone to the mall but because it was a holiday, few stores would be open. So, we did clubs. I got so anxious at a so called photography club that I had to speak to someone from SIT and it wasn't Julie. After lunch, we went to the movies. Earlier, I tried to get someone to see *Ratatouille* with me. Brent did and it was great. I think it's one of the best movies I saw in 2007.

We then went back to the camp for pizza that wasn't from the camp. During our pizza diner, Joel and Brent were talking about their sexual experiences[9]. Joel was talking about the time he "titty-fucked" and Brent talked about having a blow job. We were then dragged to see the camp's Fourth of July show, which was bad. I had told Carl that Joel and Brent got me upset with their talking. Carl told me that they could be lying, which most guys do. I decided I'd open up about my anxiety. The night was crazy. As soon as the lights went out, I heard Brent call over to Joel,

"Joel, have you cummed yet?"

---

[9] I think it bothered me because it was a bit inappropriate to be discussing at dinner and it also made me jealous. I know now that when guys do brag on about their sex lives, they are usually (or always) lying.

"No. Not yet."

This was odd. I leaned up and asked Joel if he was masturbating. He said yes and I groaned. What was sick after that is that when Joel did finally reach an orgasm, Brent walked over to his bed to see what he left. Joel did the same for Brent. I was disgusted that night.

The next morning on Day 15, we waitered but while eating I threw in the line "Last night was crazy." Joel finally told me the truth: He faked it. It was actually spit he was showing Brent. When I told this to Carl, he laughed and said that boys do these things (or something). It may've not been right to tell Carl but Chris wasn't there that day and there was no way I was telling Sammie Jo. Bekka had the day off.

Day 15 was another day of perfect stars. I tried talking to Joel during computers about my fears of socializing. He kind of got it. The night was awful. It did start out cool. I helped Neale with clubs. It was really cool to pick up things across the streets in the trailers, which looked like a living room! It was rainy but he said he was going on a hike to Toby's Rock (or something). I turned him down and decided to be with my bunk. They were in the canteen. I told Carl about my decision and he would've done the same. He said Neale does crazy things like that! Bekka also agreed too.

We then went to a stoned talent night. It was so loud that I went outside with my umbrella since it was still raining. Carl went onstage and said over mic,

"Aaron Conn, please join us when you're ready."

He then went into "My Favorite Things" and I think I had a smile on my face.

65

Day 16 was another perfect day of stars. In fact, we ranked #2 in star bunks. I remember that Carl let us ditch dance and have early showers. The evening activity was Camper-Counselor night. Joel and Brent went up with counselor Dave of ST11 and others. Joel played bass and Brent played drums for the Green Day song, "Boulevard of Broken Dreams."

When they asked me how they did, I said they were good but the way the camp presented it was awful. I didn't say it was bad. I just find it really not cool to be performing a song like a teeny-bopper thing, if you know what I mean (in other words, I took it too seriously)[10]. Joel was also there to perform the Ramones song, "Blitzkrieg Bop". I was jealous. I think I actually have a decent voice but was too shy when Neale asked days ago. Besides, I hate Green Day.

Day 17 was our seventh day of perfect stars. We practiced *Lord Of The Pants* and skipped merely to periods. The social that night got me angry. Everyone was searching for girls. I wanted to do something different and hang out with Joel and Brent but it wasn't possible. Day 18 saw the end of our streak after boating mainly due to ST10. However, I had a great day. From what I wrote, I only had one "woe-is-me" moment. We had a bunk period during fourth and watched *The Simpsons*, which was very funny. We had a unique splash night. The pool was warm, as always. I felt more connected to everyone and played ball with them in the pool. The way back was crazy. Byron changed in front of us. All the sudden, Neale came in. I laughed so hard. I even laughed when Brent accidently opened the bathroom door while I was changing. It's alright. This is the reason the boys and girls are split!

---

[10] Damn right I took it too seriously. Listen, they did a great job. I mean, given what they had at a summer camp they did a really good job. I was just flat-out jealous.

Day 19 was kind of good too. Newspaper wasn't lame and I also finished my Phil Lynott book. However, I was very angry when Joel and Brent decided to go in a paddle boat. I had asked them so many times to come with on them but they turned me down every time. They wanted to go on the banana boat or in the lake. We had clubs that night but computers was all taken up. I went back to the cabin and got a bag of gimp my sister made for me with scissors to cut the gimp. Sammie Jo had no idea what gimp was. I kind of showed her. It was something I'd do all the time at my old day camp since I had no one to talk to. Joel and I got some candy for participating the day before in everything.

Day 20 was alright I guess. We had our usual periods but the groups for the Hershey Park trip were concerning me. During swimming, Noah admitted to smoking and was forced to quit before camp started. His parents knew very little of this but didn't mind. I was creeped out! Also, people were doing anything to get on Patrick's nerves. They even flashed a camera in his face. I did yell at Brent saying that this was his only hobby and that was picking on poor Patrick. I honestly think Patrick may have autism but that's just a guess. I'm not being mean but that's the best I can describe it. I made sure he was alright and he was, just reading a book.

I also chatted to Joel about tomorrow's trip. We wouldn't be in a group since I hated rides. I asked him if we could hang at Chocolate World. Joel, who was comparing the size of his penis with Byron, said yes if I wasn't negative[11].

---

[11] That surprised me a bit. It was always the counselors who were telling me I was negative but here's Joel telling me I'm negative. As for him and Byron comparing the size of their members, it did happen. I mean one may call it completely fine but almost all the guys in the bunk were homophobic. The funny thing is that this was happening right in front of us all and no one said anything. I doubt Bekka or Sammie Jo were there.

Day 21 was the Hershey Park trip. My group was Mark and Bekka. We went to the arcades and it was fun to be with Mark. He wasn't respected by everyone in the bunk but they don't know what they're talking about. I got a Led Zeppelin chain wallet there because I was tired of carrying my money in bank paper slips.

As planned I went on the tour with Joel, Brent, and Bekka. I originally told Brandon could come with us but Joel and Brent didn't want to be with him. Brandon was okay with it.

Day 22 was a day of perfect stars. Joel told us he had a choice to stay for another session. Also, I agreed to appear in the dance show for tomorrow along with Joel and Brent. Carl and Neale showed us the dance. The song was just bunch of songs going into others. I saw the moves and just wanted to leave. The moves were so wrong that there was even a hug in it! Joel told me not to quit and I didn't. We had our pizza party that night and watched *Taladega Nights*, which wasn't bad!

Day 23 saw me becoming more jealous but we did the dance. I saw all the other dances. We can do so much better. I felt so good onstage. We had some snacks after. I even got to meet Tsur. He had just gotten back from travel. Also, I found out that Mark was going into 9th grade.

Day 24 was a perfect day of bunk stars. We shot our play too. I also helped Bekka clean the cabin for Parent's Day tomorrow. The bunk came back early and Joel and Byron came up to me. Joel then told me the good news: He was staying for full session until August 4th, which is a few days before camp ends but he has a trip to go on.

I didn't know what to say. It was just so weird. I had asked the Orb in the beginning of the year if Joel would stay longer. It said something along the line of yes. I couldn't believe it. I couldn't be happy either. So during showers, I lied down on bed with a *Survivor* buff over my head and covering my eyes. I cried silently. Colin wouldn't shut up and I told him to. Chris got angry at me. I couldn't tell him why I was angry. Early on, I told him my situation. He was willing to help me with my social skills.

Sammie finally came and I talked to her. I went to dinner without taking a shower, which I did right after dinner. My problem was that Joel was staying I wanted to be happy but I couldn't because I felt as if he wasn't treating me like a friend. I told him this before horseshoe. We agreed to hang out more, although that didn't really happen (still, Joel and I remained good friends). There was also a slideshow for session 1. I was in it five times.

Day 25 was Parents' Day. My mom, my mom's mom, my dad's parents, and my sister came to see me. I got tons of junk food, Alice Cooper's new book, and Frank Zappa's *Joe's Garage*. I kind showed them around the camp. Rebecca, my sister, went to carnival thing going on at the Horseshoe. I had my mom meet Julie, Neale, Carl, Sammie, Chris, and Bekka. My dad's parents left early and then my mom. I cried my eyes out. You can't help it. You see them once and then they leave you again.

To cheer myself up, I told Carl and Sammie I would listen to my Frank Zappa album. Zappa tends to be funny on his albums so I listened to the two-disc set. It was filled with dirty humor and it would've been a hit in the cabin had I gotten it earlier. I enjoyed the album and some of my new Alice book. By the end of the day, there were only five of us left. Brent, Brandon, Mark, Patrick, and Nolan were all on the way back home. Not only that but Chris was leaving us too. He was going to work in the kitchen. I thought he was joking but alas, he had his things all packed. There was a movie night for *Benchwarmers* but I just read and listened to music.

We woke up on Day 26 to see there were only four of us left. Colin had left early in the morning to leave for travel. It was just Byron, Noah, Joel, and I. It felt so weird. The dining hall was so empty. However during chores, Stuart and Brandon (Different from the other Brandon. I will call him either Brandon or Brandon G) of ST10 were transferred to ST11. Now there were six of us. I said hello and a simple "Welcome to the asylum!" I remember Byron giving us all Hershey candy and we had a tiny toast and celebration.

We did do our normal activities and had two bunk periods. Sammie Jo had the day off and Chris was out. I found out from Neale the new campers the day before. We were waiting for four new campers tomorrow. I found out that Stuart and Brandon were great guys. Stuart had some of the same interests as me in some way. I knew Max would be coming tomorrow. I couldn't wait for second session...but I didn't expect us to metaphorically die[12].

This ends Session 1. You may now do some pushups, jumping jacks, and all those good things before reading the rest. You may also crack your knuckles and all. Okay, enough stalling. Enjoy the rest!

Day 27 was the start of second session but for the first four periods, we were still a bunk of six. This changed during rest hour, in which we had swim instruction but it was free swim that day. I didn't have my goggles so I asked Bekka if I could get them from the cabin. She allowed me and I went up. When I got inside, I saw a new kid and his family with Sammie Jo. Sammie introduced me to Drake and we waved. I got my goggles and left to tell my bunk we had a visitor! Soon after Sammie gave Drake's family a tour of the camp, Drake came over.

---

[12] I have some explaining to do here! What I meant to say was that I didn't expect some of things that did happen. This is the best I can describe it with being a spoiler. Just a reminder: no one is going to die!

Sammie told me to talk with him and I did. I asked him his interests. He told me and he seemed like a cool kid. Oh by the way, Carl had the day off. Anyways, I saw from distance while talking to Drake a familiar face. It was Max. I waved out to him and we later said hello. I also said hi to his dad and Max got in the conversation. I was feeling good. After swimming, we had a period off. I was feeling so great that I showed some of the bunk a DVD easter egg of Yoda break dancing. They liked it. Max's bed was above mine as I requested. Also there was Joe. He was very quiet but stuck with Sammie for a while.

We had AI and then another period off. During early showers, Kevin came in back from Travel. Brandon and Stuart were delighted to see him. They all decided they should watch *Jackass 2* on Kevin's DVD player. What were they watching? Oh, just a guy getting his penis bitten by a snake. I had to leave the room. To my surprise Byron, Noah, and Joel were all out on the porch. I could tell they missed the old ST11, especially Byron. He was expecting his friend to join our bunk but he ended up in another bunk.

During dinner, Joel and I talked about the bunk just not being the same. However by the end of horseshoe, Joel had a smile his face. He had made a new friend with Kevin. I originally requested to be with Kevin since I saw a friendship starting. I was now worried as he was now getting to know Joel (what I didn't see was that this was the first day of second session. I had plenty of time!). I was mad and didn't sleep that well. Also, Colin from boating joined our cabin.

Day 28 was trip day. We had the stupid clubs first then went to the Steamtown mall again. Carl was back too! First, we went around the mall and I got some music. This included Frank Zappa's *One Size Fits All*, King Crimson's *In the Court of the Crimson King*, and Cream's *Disraeli Gears*. We then saw *Harry Potter and the*

71

Order of the Phoenix. I really liked it. I also went back to FYE to buy Queen's *Queen II*.

Day 29 was a day of perfect stars, which is impressive for a new bunk starting out. However, we had walls and ropes but it rained. With that, the next two periods were canceled and the TV was brought out. The bunk chose to watch *Epic Movie*, which I thought sucked! The evening activity was clubs for the full sessioners while the newbies had job interviews.

Day 30 was another day of perfect stars. It was cold but we did it. I played chess with Noah and made wrist bands in textiles saying my message "peace and love". However, Stuart told us something shocking with Neale present too. Stuart said he was leaving because his parents wanted him to start boarding school. You could tell in his voice he really wanted to stay so he was making a very mature decision. We all felt sorry that everyone gave him a big group hug. We also saw International Night which was so-so. I also got a Rolling Stones book in the mail that day!

Day 31 was another perfect day of stars! Sadly, Stuart left us before Period 1 began. We were now a bunk of nine. Also, the evening activity was a band that was touring camps. Their name was Julius C. Kevin was willing to come up on stage. Kids from a certain unit would at one point in the show, go up and sing a cover.

For Neale's unit, they were singing Kiss classic "Rock And Roll All Nite". I was too chicken to go up on stage. I also think it would be insulting Gene Simmons and Paul Stanley[13]. However, Kevin wanted to do it. Also, Kevin had wild ideas. His idea was to

---

[13] I don't get this. How would it be insulting? I'd be supporting Kiss! Gene and Paul (especially Gene) would've been all for me singing it. Again, I was too shy to go up on stage.

sing the song in Gene Simmons' demon make up. Being the only Kiss fan in the cabin, I offered to help with the makeup.

During Horseshoe I, along with some others, came to help. We didn't have makeup so Kevin made his own by mixing baby powder and water. Once he had that on his face, I used a Sharpie and used one of my Kiss books as reference. Also with that, he asked to wear my Kiss t-shirt. So that night, Kevin rocked and it saw the beginning of a good friendship.

Day 32 saw another day of perfect of stars. I passed my cold Delaware test. At Music, we had Karaoke. I, out of my character, sang "Hey Jude" with Kevin. Carl was proud that I got up to do that. I really did let my real voice out. Day 33 was yet another perfect day but it rained all day. So after woodshop, we went to the cabin.

I finished off my little thing called Bunkvivor. Bunkvivor was a *Survivor* with people from camp. The people would be assigned to a person from Season 14 of the show and I would shuffle pieces of paper. The final two would be a real vote. I had done 15 editions and had a winner competition (the sixteenth winner was the runner up in fifteenth). Everyone enjoyed voting off people. Sammie Jo ended up winning it against Noah, which wasn't right.

During 5th period, we were supposed to have Go Karts. The instructor allowed us go to the Nintendo Hut but it was already booked. Carl went and got a TV and I put in *Wayne's World*. I was having so much fun that I decided to skip my work period. We had a useless talent night but I just finished my Alice Cooper book and started the Stones book.

Day 34 was our official fifth perfect day of stars. We found out our unit play would be *The Wizard Of Oz*, the oldest show in the book. Kevin wanted to be the Scarecrow. With the TV still in the cabin, I put in the movie which I happened to have the three disc edition set of with me. I had a documentary put on some other time and Kevin learned a little about Ray Bolger. By studying this, he got the part! We had a trivia/reward unit night. We were in third place.

The night was so wild. No one could keep quiet so Joe (who was a nice guy but was a bad boy!) suggested we have a Truth and Dare. I had no part in this. I just watched. Joe dared Byron and Joel to "crap" together on the same toilet. They got up and did it. I could not stop laughing. Sammie heard the noise and then went into the bathroom and said,

"What? Joel and Byron, what are you doing?"

"Uh, going to the bathroom."

"Together?"

"No! Where'd you get a crazy idea like that?"

I was dying! There were other dares. Not also that but everyone could tell Kevin was masturbating under his sleeping bag. I couldn't stand it. I "kindly" threatened to go to Sammie if they didn't stop. Byron said they'd stop and the rest of the night was peaceful.

Day 35 was a stupid trip day. First off, we had a *Deal Or No Deal* game and then a period of clubs. We had our usual BBQ and then went on our trip to the Laccawana state park. There was a pool there. The girls would go in it first then the boys would, which the guys kept complaining about because they couldn't get their rocks off with someone of the other tribe.

There was a concession stand. I simply wanted a milkshake but the line was so long, it took me an hour to get one. I'm not joking. An HOUR. By this time, the boys were in the pool but had to get since there was thunder. We then got back to the camp and had out-of-camp pizza. At the table too was Joel's girlfriend Holly. Holly was a year and grade older than Joel but Joel kept saying to us he wanted to at least have a blow job from her or something. These kids were girl crazy. Where would she give it to you? There was the bathroom near the woodshop area, which was private but you couldn't get there.

We then a really stupid karaoke night on the AI field and that ended the worst trip day ever, which happened to be on Christmas in July!

Day 36 was our sixth day of perfect stars. We had our four activities but after rest hour, we went on our Delaware trip. I went on a canoe with Max and Kirsten of ST8. The bunk had a scavenger hunt for evening activity while I helped Neale with clubs. It was very funny to do clubs with him that night.

I did everything and all but G (not his real name but a nickname) from ST10 asked if his bunk can redeem their canteen prize from the *Deal Or No Deal* game. Neale said yes so Neale said we had to be quick on this. I just kept laughing. We strolled through the front office so Neale could take the key to open the canteen from the back. Neale then took a bag and filled it up with treats. He told me to get something I wanted and I did. While we were on our way out, Neale realized he forgot something important: he had to get an Italian Lemon Ice!

I later joined the bunk in the canteen and I told Carl this was my second treat. I told him about the Neale story and he laughed. It was very Neale.

Day 37 was another perfect day of stars. That day, I was laughing at most things Joe said and so was Max. Sammie was taking my laughs way to seriously. She even gave me minutes off of

Horseshoe. This wasn't the only time she got mad at me. In first session on an unknown day, I refused to switch basketball teams or something. She just said something like "You're making this difficult" and I replied "Well, good." I totally regret that because it was out of my character. She even threatened to leave in first session but of course, stayed. Anyways, it was the second Camper-Counselor night. Joel went up for something and I got pissed a little.

Day 38 marked the end of our streak after boating just like last session! Max and I went on a paddle boat, which we did most of the time during general swim (or as Carl called it "swimming generally"). I was talking to Max that he should sometime watch the Rolling Stones documentary *Gimme Shelter* with me. We wanted to watch it but Brandon, who was the only one with a DVD player that worked, said no. I told Max if we can try someone else.

We were at biking with ST10. Somehow, Max asked TJ of ST10 (who used to be with me in B15 back in Season 2) said he'd charge up his DVD player and give it to us during Horseshoe for the social. Max and I stopped by and got the DVD player with the case and remote. We could hardly hear it and somehow, it had captions. Not the DVD but the DVD player! It was almost like prostitution in a way. TJ gave us a good time and said he charged her up.

However, I had to skip a few scenes to the end (which is what you needed to see. The movie was a documentary of the Stones 1969 tour and how it ended at the Altamont Speedway. It was a free concert and Hell's Angels were the security. It got so violent that one fan was stabbed and it was caught on tape! Max later referred to this as nothing!) . The DVD player went dead and Max gave it back to TJ. I was mad but at least we saw some of it. Anyone who is reading this now please rent the movie. It is a must-see!

The night wasn't that easy but scary. Drake had done something. Mama C said she was keeping his copy of the seventh Harry Potter book till his behavior improved. Drake got so mad he threw a metal flashlight. It hit near the beds of Max and I but ended up hitting Kevin in the head. Carl, Bekka, and Sammie all heard this and quickly got Julie and another SIT and an ice pack for Kevin. It wasn't funny but crazy.

Day 39 was oddly a perfect day of stars! We didn't have any periods off. It got crazy at ceramics, even from the beginning when the instructor told us we would use balls of clay. Yeah, go ahead and laugh. Balls. I was shocked to find out that Noah, Max, Joel, and Drake were all going into 9th grade. I knew about Joel and Drake earlier though. Joe wouldn't say but he was 14 then. When you're 14, you're usually starting 9th grade. Kevin, Brandon, and I were all going into 10th and Byron was going into 11th. We had our ice cream party and watched *Monty Python And The Holy Grail*.

Day 40 wasn't special but had some moments that were bad. Sammie gave me five minutes off of Horseshoe for nothing. I didn't care. All I do during there is listen to music and burn calories. Also, we had go-karts and I was bored. When I got bored, I'd usually ask Carl to entertain me. Noah told me to stop whining all the time and Byron and Joel agreed with him. I was pissed. I talked to Carl and told him I was hurt emotionally. I was just making a joke because I was bored. I honestly wanted to throw a rock in Noah's face and say "Fuck you!". However, I couldn't. I'd get in trouble and I'd lose my family rating for this paper, which I've already done.

Day 41 was a day of perfect stars. We were out of control in Discovery. Simon even threatened to not give us perfect stars. Just because you live with a certain specialist doesn't mean you'll always get perfect stars with him (or for the girls, her). However that night, Simon read the first parts of the Roald Dahl classic *The BFG*. He read it in his great voice and then had voices for all the characters. Some people listened but I recorded it and died of laughter.

Day 42 was the day of our Dorney Park trip. We would've been at the Wayne County Fair but since camp started so early, Dorney would have to come first since the WCF didn't start yet. I was in a combined group. My real group was Carl, Max, and Noah with Bekka, Kevin, and Drake. It was fun. We went to arcades and a few cheap rides. I found the restaurant, Game Day, from last year. I suggested to Carl and Bekka we have our dinner there because lines would be crowded if we had dinner at the planned time. They agreed and we had some good food. Joe didn't come on the trip with us since he had really bad behavior.

Day 43 was Track and Field Day, which is my least favorite day on camp. We were the blue team and I had doubts on winning. What is weird is that the team that I end up on won the year before. I didn't have any blue t-shirts but only a blue *Survivor* buff. So, I wore Alice Cooper makeup in blue. Sammie hated Alice Cooper but I guess some people liked it. They were kind of confused though.

As I predicted, we didn't win. We came in third, red came in second, and white came in first. I also started to see that day that Joel was becoming lazy during meals. He would always have some kind of excuse not to eat what was on the table. He was going home soon so yeah…

Day 44 remains a very weird day indeed. We had a trip, then Track & Field, and now the unit play. This was all in one swallow. It wasn't easy. I decided to take part in the dance our bunk was doing for *Oz* no matter how stupid it was. The first period was canceled due to the weather I think and then I had work. For third and fourth period, we practiced the dance. Carl took Joel, Noah, Brandon,

Kevin, and I to the canteen for good behavior. Max had work but I made sure my buddy got his treats.

During rest hour, there were only six of us in the cabin. Joe was on Neale's porch, Kevin was practicing, and Drake had threatened earlier to leave by walking home. We tried to watch *Ace Ventura* then *Sliders* in the cabin, which most of us got hooked on. Unfortunately, we had to waiter in bad weather for dinner. The power went out a few times and dinner was put on hold. It was very stressful.

Before more practice in the Rec Hall, Carl had to talk to us. He told us that Drake was staying despite his episode. Joe, however, was going home tomorrow. Regina wanted him out and his parents wanted to see if camp helped him. It didn't and we didn't see him that night.

We all knew that this was Joel's last night. There were many people sad about Joel leaving. I was kind of sad and Sammie asked me if I was. At the time, I told her I didn't know what to say. I still hadn't felt that Joel had treated me like a friend. As I mentioned before, Joel and I are still good friends. I just didn't know how to react then.

On the morning of Day 45, Joel left ST11. He said goodbye to every one of us and that was that. It felt weird not having him there. Joe also left that day but slept in the nurses the night before. This quickly dwindled ST11 down to seven campers: Byron, Noah, Kevin, Max, Brandon, Drake, and I. That night was our *Oz* play and it was surprisingly good. I think Carl had then night off.

Also, some more attempts at bonking the girls were made. Noah knew this girl from across our bunk named Lindsey. He really liked her. After horseshoe, Noah gave this baseball innuendo version. I asked him outside about what he did. He told me he fingered Lindsey. Noah told me to keep it a secret and to "pinky" promise. I did the goddamn pinky thing and God knows where that pinky had been.

Day 46 saw us having a normal day. We had a lie in like we do on Saturdays or Sundays. However, our rest period is taken away and put in place is a swim instruction. We ditched music. Noah had his normal outbursts. I don't talk about them in this because they were an ongoing thing. We had a movie night with *Napoleon Dynamite* but I just listened to Alice.

Day 47 was a perfect stars day. Noah had more moments and I went to computers during Horseshoe. We saw two terrible unit plays for *The Little Mermaid* and *Spiderman*. Day 48 started out normal till periods three and four. We saw the last of the unit plays *TMNT* and *The Muppet Show*. Sammie Jo, once again, gave me time off for Horseshoe. However, there were some laughs for our last discovery period which involved Mild Duds. Kevin had so many in his mouth what the chocolate was drooling from his mouth. It was somewhat funny but nasty too.

Day 49 was our last trip day. However in the middle of the might, I got sick and asked for Carl. I felt warm and he gave me some crackers and juice from the reward box (or which I called the Magic Box). When I woke up, I still felt terrible. Instead of clubs, the STs had a Round Robin in the hot sun. It was for an ice cream party. I wasn't feeling well and I napped with some Alice on. When I wasn't tired, I got up and went to the bathroom. I noticed I was a bit dizzy.

Still, I got well enough to go to the Wayne County Fair. My group was Max and Bekka. I started to worry about the end. We then split up. The boys went to a baseball game while the girls went to the mall. That got me pretty pissed off because I would've honestly gotten some more music but I had a money plan to buy certain things after camp so it would ruin that. The game was alright but I was feeling shaky and tense about the end.

Day 50 was a perfect day again. There was one incident that happened that day. Byron, Noah, and I were all at the waterfront. I found a page to the staff *Mary Poppins* play. I told them this would be the play and then proceeded to imitate what Tim would say. Noah then ended that with,

"Now you can all go and have sex…except Aaron, who can't get a girlfriend."

I wasn't offended at first but later on, I wanted to kill him. Both he and Byron were puzzled that a boy my age at 15 didn't have a girlfriend or dated once. The Prom was that night and was cheesy. We had a banquet and I had my hair nice and a Rolling Stones vest thing with it. However, Sammie Jo didn't allow me to bring any electronics or books. When I'm there, I see other kids with their stuff. What the hell?

We also found out that our unit won Round Robin. I felt happy but I wasn't a part of that. Drake said that if I didn't get any ice cream, he refused to eat his. That says something. I even prayed for us to win!

Day 51 was rainy that we watched *Mission: Impossible III* and all. We swam in the steamed pool. I also started to pack and talked to Julie about my year in short. We also saw the staff *Mary Poppins* play. It was great.

Day 52 was like any other day but wasn't towards the end. We had boating and I was with Sammie Jo in a row boat. Colin came over on the speed boat thingy and drenched Sammie and I as requested by Carl. I was so pissed off. All the way, I kept throwing F bombs left and right. Carl finally got me to stop and apologized. He really meant to get Sammie. I accepted it and lived on.

The slideshow for second session was cool and I was in it six times. We then went to the waterfront and had the burnout. There were kids crying that it was the end. I would have shed a tear but I couldn't. At every burnout, I cry. This one, I didn't and I even tried. I couldn't. I think I was relieved that it was all over. Still, it was sad to leave.

Day 53 was the last day logically. We had breakfast and as soon as we were done, there wasn't really any time to sit down and relax and wait for the bus. The bus to Philadelphia was leaving early. I gave Max a hug and all my counselors a hug. Byron went with me on the bus. Before I got on, Carl said thanks for another great year and good luck. I almost cried my eyes out but I was strong. Once we got to the place, I was one of the first to get off. Byron said goodbye and told me to keep the recordings I made! I left home with my mom. Like always, it felt weird to be back in the real world. My sister was still at her camp and she returned a few days later. I was worried about moving on…

After camp ended, I've had some contact with my bunkmates. I instant message Brent frequently. I also have Brent and Joel as friend on MySpace. I met Max twice before 2007 ended. I went over to his house first and then he came over to my house.

As for my counselors, I have yet to keep in contact with them. I may email Carl one of these days. Who knows? What I know is that I told my story in two days in the new year of 2008. Speaking of 2008, I will be returning to camp for my fifth year and I'll stay full session once again. I'm good until my sixth year, which might be my last in 2009. However, I'm one that doesn't want to look too far into the future and not think too much about the past.

Overall, my fourth year was different from my previous year. I had two returning people (Carl and Neale) and made some new friends, which I hope I really did. I had two good sessions and they both ended on happy notes. This year also showed me I can soldier on without the people I was with since my very first day. It showed me that there are at least some people out there who like me and showed me a year without my former closest friend there. As I wait for my fifth year, I'd like to look back on my fourth year as a very good year.

THE END!

The Camp: Season 5
By Aaron Conn

I did enjoy my fourth year at Summit Camp and did have a good time. However, I was down on myself during that year. I already decided to go back again for the whole session. This year was mature, immature, and fun. Little did I know, I would be lonely during the second half. This is my fifth year of camp!

Preface

Once again, this preface is necessary! After a long fourth year, I continued with my life. I started my school year as a sophomore in September. It was a challenging year. It wasn't as good as my freshman year but still, I did great. Still, I was anxious. The Trent incident was history for me so I could sleep better. I tried my best to be social around others. In school, I was completely mute.

Despite this, I was able to interview four people related to music. These people were Yoko Ono, Rudy Sarzo, and Steve Holly. The fourth was Kelly Garni, who I interviewed a day before camp started.

I was already prepared for my fifth year. Previously, I wrote my traditional letter. Regina gave me a rough list of kids who I'd be with. I also asked to be with a certain counselor: Carl. I was disappointed with last year counselor wise. One day, the phone rang and my mom answered. It was Neale, who would be my unit leader for the third time. However, Neale didn't want to speak with me. My mom said to check my email and I immediately got to my computer. Neale told me that Carl was returning and that I would be with him again! I couldn't believe it. I was going to have Carl and Neale again? This was too good to be true.

Neale did explain why he couldn't speak with me. The reason was because being the age of 16; I was old enough to go to camp without talking to anyone over the phone. Although I was disappointed, I understood and just left it as that.

I had called Max two days before I left. He would be with me again and told me that a guy named Simon would be one of our counselors. This wasn't his first year. Last year, Simon worked in computers. Although confused, I was excited to be with Carl, Neale, Max, Joel, Brandon, and Kevin again.

It was June 26th, 2008. I left for the same hotel with my mom and my paternal grandmother. I was nervous and let Noel of Adventure know that. I did see Patrick from last year and said hello. He didn't know which bunk he was in but he didn't end up with me.

The trip to camp was fine. I was nervous that when I got there, Carl wouldn't be there. When we got there, the bus went on the horseshoe. I was the last one off as they forgot to call my name or bunk! The guy that was waiting for me was Simon and helped me carry my stuff. He led me to the cabin, which was on the horseshoe. I asked him if Carl was there.

"Yeah, he's waving at you."

I looked up to see Carl jumping up and down and waving to me. He ran up, gave me a hug, and said hello. When I got in the cabin, Carl spotted my bed. Next to me was Joel, who was playing his acoustic guitar in bed. Max would sleep above me once again. I later said hello to my female counselor named Carol. She was from Scotland and this was her first year.

So, we all just chatted and I also gave Carl a gift: *The Number 7*, his first album I made which had recordings of the two years I had him. He kept laughing at the cover and thanked me for the gift. Julie also came over and said hello. Kevin, Joe, Glenn, and Aldan all came later. Brandon was already there. So once there were eight of us Carl, Simon, and Carol all spoke to us. Dinner would be soon and they told us that the ninth camper, Seth, would be coming tomorrow. After dinner was Horseshoe, in which I walked around talking to Max. I bumped into Neale, who I already met. Still he said,

"You still haven't given me a hug."

I did so and I told that the kids were all getting smaller! I felt kind of huge. Next, we had our social. Like all other socials, I thought nothing of it. By the end of day, I felt left out. Joel, Joe, Kevin, and Glenn all really got along since they knew each other the year before. I tried to think positive and just thought that they would get used to me and like me.

At bed time, Carol had to take our food. Minutes later, she came back with it and told us that we could keep it in the cabin. Carol told us we're the oldest bunk and most mature bunk on camp. I told her this was great because I'm a bit of a picky eater!

Day 2 saw our bunk, ST12, at our best. We started with mountain biking followed by camp crafts. During computers, Seth arrived. He seemed like a nice kid from first impressions but we would all wait and see. We then waitered for lunch. My table this year was GST5.

We had been told early on by Neale that there wouldn't be any general swim because they were testing the younger kids first. Somehow, Neale was misinformed and we did the tests. It was hell. I was so dizzy from swimming in the lake. With no relaxation, we went to AI. It was very dirty because we were playing all these games in which we'd have to touch each other!

Video Arts was nice while dance was dirty because we played some game. The game was to do these things when the instructor called them or you're out of the game. Max and I actually won and at the end of the day, we had perfect stars. I couldn't believe it. That night we saw Steven Max, the guy who plays Simon Says and balances things on his face. At bed time, I spoke with Simon and Carol outside about my anxiety. Carl had told them about it early on but I told them more about it. I felt so comfortable and I slept great that night.

Day 3 was another perfect day of stars. Neale had the day off so Carl had his first day as deputy. Deputies are the counselors who take over the job of a unit leader when they're not on camp. I did get to use my recorder and get some stuff.

Early on, I planned on Carl having another album made. However, Carl refused to be recorded. Now, he was really busy that day so I tried not to bother him much. Carl said he'd sing only if I did my 25 laps, which is hell. The only time I had done my 25 laps was in 2006. When you do your 25 laps, you can go in a kayak or a sailboat in boating. I only went on a kayak once that year. So, I never bothered with it until now.

I did note in my journal that I thought that the bunk was starting to crack. I was so wrong about that but the reason why I wrote that was because that day, Joe asked the Orb if Aldan was gay. God love Joe but that's just not right. I think I was also trying to find something to make me upset!

I sometimes felt left out when it came to the friendship of Joel and Kevin. During the lame camp fire we had that night, Joel and Kevin were making early plans for the Camper-Counselor night this session. I was so pissed because I had something in mind already. I talked to Simon and he helped me a little. I just had to chill out.

Day 4 saw our third perfect day of stars. The first few periods that morning were basketball, ceramics with our specialist Jon, and swim instruction. During this morning, I was telling Carl about my anger from last night. I wanted to stand up this year and do something for the talent night this session.

I personally wanted to do "Cum On Feel The Noize" by Quiet Riot. Why that song? Back in November the singer of the band, Kevin DuBrow, suddenly passed away which left me depressed for a month. I felt this was sort of a dedication to him, although I had shown enough respect for him!

Luckily, I was able to pull Joel and Kevin aside that day and tell them what I wanted to do. They said they'd be on board if I had the tablature for guitar and bass. I felt so good. We were laughing so much that day.

During rest hour and fifth period Max, Kevin, and I watched *The Naked Gun*. During Walls and Ropes, we played mind games. Aldan took things way to seriously and said that it was my fault that we couldn't tie a knot. Joel, Joe, Max, and Seth all stood up for me.

All day long, Joel had a milk carton with some stuff in there. He and Joe took turns shaking it and trying to make butter! We called the carton Mickey for some odd reason! The carton was getting weak so we put it in a water bottle that had a clip on it to put on your pants or shorts. By horseshoe, it had failed but that didn't stop Carl and Carol (Simon had the day off). When I'd go out on the porch during horseshoe that day, I heard Carl say in a Scottish accent,

"I'm churning some butter."

We all laughed and Carl got so crazy that day. He was so crazy that he and Neale sang "You've Lost That Loving Feeling" on the recorder. It was wild. Still, that night was lame. We had a *Transformers* night and I just wrote in my other journal and listened to music. As noted in my journal, I was still jealous. I don't know why.

Day 5 was our fourth perfect day of stars. We felt as if we could keep going with this. Carol had the day off. Nothing much happened except that we had our Delaware tests. It wasn't as bad as I thought it was going to be.

Arts and Crafts was so funny because with only the instructor and Simon present, we made a special flag of Ireland for Carl. In the middle of the white stripe was a drawing of Carl's biggest fear: a coil fish! We put glue-on eye on the fish. I wrote the words and everyone signed it. Simon even put a quotation bubble and inside it he wrote,

"I love Irish boys!"

Before AI, we had our bunk photo. We waitered for dinner that night and Max and I got to go to computer during horseshoe time and clubs. Joel also told me that the Quiet Riot song was hard to play and that song used distortion, which the camp didn't have. I immediately suggested that the song should now be "Sweet Jane" by the Velvet Underground. It was easier and we agreed to that. Constantly that day, people were commenting how skinny I was. I hadn't got comments like that since I was ten years old.

Day 6 saw the end of our streak. It ended last period thanks to the very immature ST11. Still, it was a great day. We had karate, circus, and swimming instruction. I tried to be funny at waitering when we were trying to pass down dirty silverware, when I said something on the lines of shut up but with humor. Aldan took it too personally. Joe pulled me aside and said,

"Aaron if he throws anything, let me know."

Hey, I got a back-up team! Still, I would tell Carl, Simon, or Carol of this. By the way, Carl had the day off. The evening activity was fun. We had to go in our cabin and put 26 things in that started with the 26 letters of the alphabet. We got second place and chose the Nintendo Hut with canteen treats. I was very proud of my item for Q: a Quiet Riot shirt.

Day 7 was our first trip day and/or day off. However, we had the stupid clubs program in the morning before the trip. We had a game in the unit where we had to construct a small catapult. We then had free swim in the pool.

When I was in the pool, Carol wanted to see if I could do a handstand. I said I would need ear plugs for the water, which the staff had. The head of the Waterfront, Debbs, gave me two wax ear plugs. When I put them in, I found out one of them was too small and deep in. Carl said to get out of the pool. I had the one in my left ear out. Debbs checked to see if she had any tweezers.

Meanwhile, Neale and the counselors were having a field day asking me if I could hear them. Debbs found a safety pin and was able to get it out, in which everyone clapped for. Slightly embarrassed, I decided to sit out for the rest of the period!

Next, we had our BBQ on the AI field. We than went to the Steamtown Mall area. My group was Simon, Max, and Seth. From what I wrote, we went to FYE first and I got four albums. They were

Black Sabbath's *Heaven and Hell*, Bob Dylan's *Blood On The Tracks*, Judas Priest's *Painkiller*, and Lou Reed's *Transformer*.

When we went to the theater across the street and had a choice of movies early on. My group went to see *WALL.E*, which was great. It's one of those movies that campers are too shy to pick because they're worried that they're not cool enough. I just stated I like to watch good movies. Being that the movie had Pixar's name on it, I wanted to see it.

For the only time, we were on a bus with Neale. He told us that we would be playing a game called the One Dollar Challenge. What you needed to do was buy the most random thing that'll come as no use. The trick was that it needed to be a dollar or less. I didn't participate but others did.

On the ride back to camp, Kevin' submission of a Jesus nightlight won. As a prize, you got all of the things that were given. Oddly enough, I had found on the ground at camp that day an English coin. My counselors were telling me that if you gave it to someone else, the luck continues. Kevin wanted it and I gave it to him. Kevin was nice enough to give out the crap he won to us. I was allowed to have a road atlas from 2004!

Day 8 was rainy. Into third period, it started to pour. We did, however, go to music. Instead of having discovery after rest hour, we had Tribes in the bunk with Julie. Neale was also with us. We were supposed to go to swim instruction but it started to rain again. The waterfront staff invited us to the canteen to have treats.

During this time I listened to the rest of the new things I bought the day before, having already heard the Lou Reed album last night. Hockey was canceled also. The funny thing about hockey this

91

year is that we never went there and kept canceling it. So let me put it straight that ST12 were never seen at hockey.

Carl managed to get a TV from Neale's room. He tried to get one with a DVD player but all that was left was a VHS player. Max and I went down with Carl to the HC Hut to pick out a movie. We picked *Billy Madison*. It had been years since I saw this! We had a lame talent night but canteen was nice. I finally got to talk to our specialist, Jon. He is really cool. I did note in my journal that Seth's laugh was on my nerves and that he'd laugh at anything.

Day 9 started off really rough. At breakfast, we all sat at the table wherever. I was sitting next to Seth. The ST12 table, which was the ST11 table last year, was two tables long like every other table. So, we'd have to use our manners and ask for food to be passed to us. However, Seth was yelling in my ear. I'd be enjoying my meal until I heard,

"PASS THE WATER, PLEASE!"

Jeez, man! You got to lower the hell down. We started the day with mountain biking and camp crafts. Camp crafts was first and we had to make a shelter using the branches and leaves in the woods we were walking in. Brandon, Max, and I were one group. Out of the three groups, our group had the best shelter!

I didn't want to go biking but Carl gave me no choice. However while I was biking, I stepped into a puddle of mud. My shoes were ruined and the left one was soaked. Luckily, I had another pair of shoes to wear. After waitering, we had our rest hour robbed from us like we do every Friday for general swim and/or boating. I did, however, save Carol and Max in the row boat we were in!

AI was terrible because none of the boys in the unit got any rest. Video Arts was cool because we were in front of a green screen but we never saw those shots. Dance was off and was for the rest of the year. Friday was always the camp special, which was always in the Rec Hall. Dance was held in the Rec Hall but during seventh period, people would have to practice. So that was out. We then decided to take early showers.

However, Aldan hadn't done his chore this morning to ask for more towels. Seth had his own towel so he was walking naked all over the place, which we always hated. His excuse was that we were all guys. That might be true but there are many of us who don't want to see anything hiding under your pants! There weren't any counselors. Simon and Joel were sick. I tried to take lead with the people that were there until towels came.

Also that day, our laundry got mixed up with ST11's who decided they should throw our clothes in their cabin. Jeez, they are so smart! That night was the Fourth of July special, which was alright. Aldan and I didn't see the fireworks and we went to the canteen with Mama C, who I forgot to say was back this year also. I remember that Aldan started talking with Hillary of GST8, the first session girlfriend of last year's Nick. Nick was supposed to come this year but didn't.

Day 10 saw us back to perfect stars. We started off the day making cookies in home economics. Woodshop followed while Carol, Max, and I were in a row boat again! At boating, I overheard another bunk talking to one other camper about getting a girlfriend. From the start, I thought the idea of dating in camp was so stupid. During AI, I decided that in rest hour I should write a song. I did with Kevin helping. I called the song "Kosher Kisses", teasing about how stupid the dating is at Summit Camp, which is also kosher. I couldn't write it alone so Kevin was there and we agreed to any line he suggested.

For the most part, I wrote the song. Having two people working together can have creative juices flowing. Joel came up with the music towards the end of first session and we recorded four versions of it on my recorder. Nature was cool because while on a walk, I discovered the shelter ST11 made last year. Carl, who had his deputy day, came by and petted one of the rabbits. It was too funny because he was kind of scared! He also bumped his head after trying to get himself out of the cage!

Soccer was sweaty while Go-Karts was cool. That night was a social but I just wrote in my black journal. I think by the end of that day, most of the bunk had heard me sing "Kosher Kisses". Joe told me to write a song about how much he eats. I never finished it.

Day 11 saw another perfect day of stars. Notably, I did my 25 laps just so I could have Carl sing and happiness for me. While swimming, I was trying to think positive. Who would be proud of me? First person that came to my mind was my late and great dad. I did the 25 laps and while using the towel to dry off, a butterfly landed on my legged on the towel. Glenn pointed out that if a butterfly lands on you, it means you have a gentle heart. That got me because I once said that I thought my dad passed away because he had a good heart, since my family doesn't know how he went. In this messed up world, those people have to go too soon.

Before waitering, I was too choked up so I had to talk to Carl. I began to cry and tell him I was thinking of my dad. Carl was saying he would be proud. I couldn't believe something like this would get me upset. Usually at times like this, I'd suck up. Not this time.

During my work period at newspaper, I had planned to write an article on the forty summers Summit Camp was celebrating. I wanted to interview Mayer, the man who started the camp with his wife in 1969. To arrange this, I'd have to talk to the head counselor and announcer at meal times, Tim Kedge. The HC Hut asked me to pick my least favorite activity for tomorrow. I said sixth period, which was AI. The appointment was set! That night we had a splash night with Neale and ST11.

Day 12 saw our third perfect day on our second streak. One of the highlights on that day was going on a rowboat with Brandon, Joel, and Neale. I was kind of jealous of the relationship between Joel and Neale. I felt as if Neale was playing favorites. I knew he wasn't. During our shortened rest period and fifth period, I was able to play *The Naked Gun 2 ½* on Kevin' DVD player.

Then at sixth period, I talked with Tim. He shook my hand and I told him that most of my questions were for Mayer but I still did ask him a few questions. Tim told me to have one of my counselors to speak with Mayer and arrange a time to talk. He asked me the name of one of my counselors. I mentioned Carl. The funniest thing that happened was when I asked him what year he came to camp. He looked up at the ceiling and thought. I said,

"The site says you came in 1978 as a counselor."

"That might be right." Tim said.

When Max asked me how the interview went, I tried to be humorous and said in a frightened voice,

"He wouldn't stop touching me…how do you think it went?"

Max just stared at me but he laughed and got it, I think. I think Max is one of the very few people to understand my sense of humor. Also that morning Neale had to talk to Joel, Kevin, and I. He said the song that we wanted to do, "Sweet Jane", wouldn't be possible because Tim and other big heads wouldn't allow music such as this. We had to come up with something else.

First thing that came out of my mouth was "Jumpin' Jack Flash". I think I remember Kevin wanting it to now be a Rolling Stones song. I then suggested that we do "You Can't Always Get What You Want" because it was released on the Stones album *Let It Bleed*, which came out in 1969 just like Summit did. In fact, the song was the B-side of "Honky Tonk Women", which became a hit that summer. Neale, Kevin, and Joel liked the idea.

Max, however, felt left out and said he wanted to help out in some way. I joked around at first that he could be a groupie! Then I seriously thought he *could* be a part of this. Max said he wanted to be a part of something. I suggested him to sing backing vocals. He agreed and so did Kevin and Joel.

Day 13 was our fourth perfect day. Drama started off the morning and that was fun. During rest hour, Joel and I practiced "You Can't Always Get What You Want". Newspaper saw me all confused. The instructor, Sandra, pointed out I should be at certain periods which weren't on my schedule. Some of those periods weren't possible because I would have to waiter lunch. I told Neale about this and he said he'd do something.

Boating was interesting. I was in a row boat with Lucas of ST11. He seemed friendly when I first met him at basketball on Day 4 I think it was. He stuck out, for me, as the coolest of ST11. After we were on the boat, I tried to talk with him. We kind of hung out during the last minutes. I found out he was a grade younger than me.

I was thinking that Lucas could be the first out-of-bunk friend. I thought about going to see him at horseshoe time but he was with his girlfriend, Hillary, who wasn't Aldan's girlfriend yet.

That night was an out-of-pool splash night. What did this mean? Would they be getting out pump-up pools? No, we would just be playing four very wet games and run around on the AI field. We didn't win but the winning team got to pour a whole trash can worth of cold water on Neale, who was fully clothed. Neale did come by to our cabin and said something like his "nut-sack" was shrunken but he'll be fine. Thanks for sharing, Neale!

Day 14 was our second trip day. We did the morning clubs. I went to computers then an all-girl Bingo, which was weird because the STs were going to have a Bingo night after the trip! We had our BBQ then went to the movies. I saw *Hancock*, which was alright. We then went to Wal-Mart. My group was Carl, Glenn, and Seth.

The music selection was like hell. It was almost all compilations. Still out of the pits of this hell, I bought Def Leppard's *Hysteria* and Metallica's *Master of Puppets*. We then had regular horseshoe then off-camp pizza at camp.

We then had to get ready for Bingo night. We had to have a theme and dress up. Joel suggested we all go as track runners, wearing headbands and short shorts. Joel was our mascot and it was too funny. I just got one of my *Survivor* buffs as the headband and then pulled up the shortest shorts I had. We looked too funny. Max was able to win stand-up Bingo and get us all cups of 7 Up. Glenn got a beach towel and Joel and Kevin got $15 gift cards to Wal-Mart. I didn't get shit. Oh well.

Day 15 was our fifth perfect day of stars but this day was a hard one. For the first four periods of the day Max, Brandon, Simon,

97

and I went on the Delaware with other people from Neale's Unit. We then had discovery, where we had to make a design of a flying machine. Carol paired me up with Seth. Seth was too negative and I myself wanted to be with Max but he had a work period.

I participated creating a design with the plates and sticks we were given. The wings I wanted to look like moustaches and have straws hanging out the plate. A balloon was on top to finish it. Thinking of Frank Zappa, I called the thing Fido!

After discovery, Neale pulled us aside. He told us that Glenn had been at Regina's because he did something out-of-character. So he spoke with his parents and they decided he would go home. However, Glenn is mature so there was a chance of him coming back for second session. Still, the remaining eight of us were upset. Compared to Kyle of last year, this was a guy I actually liked. It felt empty without him.

We had water games in swim instruction. We then had to clean up and all. I was crying because Carol put too much pressure on me, saying I'd have to have last showers and do two chores tomorrow because of something. Carol said she didn't want to see me upset and let me go to the shower so I wasn't late for practice. At practice, the instructor and everyone were giving me way too many suggestions. I think Joel said that day,

"Do you know how much pussy you'll get after this?"

I just laughed and said it wasn't allowed! Later that night, we had trivia night.

Day 16 was six days of perfect stars. During chores, we all practiced and I got to the point where I **had it** with suggestions. These things included singing from the diaphragm and standing up straight and looking alive. I was going to explode into tears and let Carol know this. She left Joel, Kevin, and Max behind when we went to mountain biking and camp crafts. Joel and Kevin were cool with me and understood my worries.

We had normal periods except starting from this day till the last day we would have a laundry period. We all helped each other folding and giving the laundry. Video Arts got me jealous because I didn't feel part of the project. Carl came over to listen us perform since he had the night off. We were the second act onstage that night. We were to go on as Neale's Band but I preferred Neale's Children. Joel was on guitar, Kevin was on bass, Gordon of ST10 was on drums, Elan of ST10 was on cello, Max was on backing vocals, and I was lead vocals.

We performed "You Can't Always Get What You Want" and managed to make a seven minute song into a four minute song. From what I heard after, my microphone wasn't on for the first minute or first few seconds. When we finished, I said thanks to the crowd and they all clapped. Julie and Neale were both proud and liked my hair since I didn't have my Doors hat on. I was so proud.

Day 17 was our seventh perfect day of stars. I wasn't feeling good that morning. At woodshop, I literally napped outside. It was so hot and I had my water fan. Kat from Nature suggested in an attempt of earning stars, tell the instructor that we'd like to have the activity in the bunk and still get stars. We followed that advice for soccer and watched some of *The Naked Gun 33 1/3*.

Dinner was so funny. Our table was close to the window which was infested with bugs. So, we sat at an empty B18 table. It was too weird. The B18 sign wasn't even hanging from the ceiling. During announcements, I found the sign and when first bunks were called I slid it to the front of the table and they held up high for Tim to read. It worked and we were second out!

During horseshoe, I helped Kevin look like Alice Cooper since he would be performing with Joe and some other boys of the unit with Julius C, who came last year second session. They sang "I Love Rock N Roll" by Joan Jett and rocked. The song choice was weird to begin with. Neale chose two female songs for us. We chose the Joan Jett one over "I Will Survive". Since I was happy with the night before, I decided not to go onstage that night.

Day 18 was our eighth perfect day of stars. During first period, it rained so we went to the new Wii Hut. During swim instruction, I got depressed. I didn't say why in my journal. Walls and Ropes was nice and we left a little early and had showers. I was the first in the shower since I had to interview Mayer. Carol took me to the office and when we got there, Mayer said I could come in. He was very nice and had so much information.

That night, it was raining badly. So, we had a cereal and treats night in the cabin to watch *Dumb and Dumber*. During this, Jed of ST11 visited our bunk. He was mainly talking to Brandon and Aldan. At first, I didn't like Jed. He said that night,

"Wouldn't that be cool if we were all in a bunk together?"

I just thought "Dream on".

Day 19 saw nine days of perfect days. That morning was bad for me. During chores, I was joking to Max about how playing the guitar isn't the way to go. Join the dark side and be a journalist! Aldan said something negative about "your daddy". I immediately flipped Aldan off and walked out the door furious. Carl wanted to know what was wrong and I told him that Aldan better watch his mouth. Carl said he would speak to Aldan and Carl was sure that Aldan would feel bad.

We did make finger puppets in textiles that day. I made Kiss finger puppets! Arts and Crafts had us joined with Neale and AI was somehow funny. During showers, we finished *Dumb and Dumber*. We even saw Tim's brother visiting the camp with his nephew. Clubs that night was lame but we got back to the cabin and started to trash celebrities!

Day 20 saw us tying the record that Carl, Max, and I had in 2006 which was ten days of stars. Martial Arts was brutal and circus was good. During that time, I found out that Carol knew who Jimmy McCulloch was. Jimmy McCulloch was the guitarist for Paul McCartney & Wings from 1974 to 1977 and died in 1979. When I tried thinking of Scottish musicians, I mentioned his name and Carol said she heard of him because there aren't too many famous people coming out of Scotland.

During third period Max, Joel, Joe, Kevin, and I all met up with Neale to practice and come up with ideas for our dance for the dance show. In the Fourth of July show, there was a fake boy band named Boyforce. They lip-synched a bunch of songs together and it was funny. We were going to be the teenage equivalent. We had to come up with a name and I was suggesting Boytallica like Metallica. Everyone liked Joel's idea which was Boy Division like Joy Division. Still, it ended up as Boyforce Jr. We would be lip-synching "Tearin' Up My Heart" by N'SYNC and dancing.

I was able to finish my article that day but both general swim and baseball were lame. The evening activity that night was rules for Dorney Park, where we would have our third trip. This wasn't normal as we usually had Hershey Park as the big trip for first session.

101

Day 21 was our trip day for Dorney Park. It was kind of fun. My group was Carol and Max joined with Simon, Kevin, and Seth. The only thing I went on was a pretty lame swan boat ride. They were like the paddle boats at camp except these things had big swans on them! When everyone went on one ride, I was hanging out with Neale. He was too funny and too random since he asked me,

"So Aaron, do you think black people get sunburn?"

I was just laughing and thinking "What the heck?" We did see the dance show *Heat*. Carl and unit leader Steve were crazy during the show. It was a bunch a dancers dancing and singing to today's hits and some oldies. Carl and Steve were crazy because they too were dancing in their seats! The dance show had my mind in the gutter. That show had more sexual innuendos than a boy bunk on camp!

My group also went to Game Day for our early dinner. Another funny thing that happened was when I made my weekly call to Alice Cooper, Carl spoke to him and requested for Alice to play "…Baby One More Time" by Britney Spears. I ended the call by telling Alice not to play the song. He wouldn't have any way!

Day 22 was a historic day: we beat the record and got eleven perfect days of stars! The morning was boring but practice with Neale was so funny. He would even swear from time to time. We were shocked by this with him being a unit leader and all. He said,

"I feel like you guys are us. I mean when I'm done going from cabin to cabin, I say 'How the fuck are you?!'"

We pretty much had a chilled day. Nothing much happened except I newly named Be A Star Night the name Acid Trip Night!

Day 23 was our twelfth perfect day of stars! Everything was going good until our laundry period.

At the end of our laundry period, Brandon discovered two mice in this bag. We all freaked when they started to crawl on the floor. When the guys were able to get the first one out, I stood on the shoe bin outside. We drew attraction in the horseshoe. Carl and Simon were there after their weekly seminar.

Upon hearing of the mice, Carl ran over to the porch of ST11. I asked if I could join him but he said I was braver! The problem was that most of the bunk saw two mice. One of them was in the bathroom. Also, Carol told us she had Lyme's Disease. Despite this, we had tribes.

That night was the Dance Show. Neale lend us some snap jackets so we could take them off and throw them into the crowd. I was given a white beater (also known as a wife beater!). I think when everyone saw me in that, I looked great. I also had one of Neale's hats on too. We were the second ones on and it was so much fun. Kelvin, one of my very few surviving counselors left on camp, was proud of Max and me.

Day 24 was the thirteenth day of perfect stars for us. We only had woodshop, general swim, and nature. After nature, we had a party in the cabin. There was pizza, soda, and candy. We also put in a movie, which was *Rat Race*. Before this, I revealed the winner of the Bunkvivor winners round. If you remember last year, Bunkvivor was something I did for fun. This time, I was only using counselors. The final two this time was Simon and Carol. Carol won after a 5-2 vote. We also had to get the bunk clean for tomorrow, which was parent's day.

We also saw the first session slideshow. Even before the slideshow started, they were having trouble with getting the projector to work. So, Regina filled up time by singing her anthem "You Are My Sunshine". Next, Mayer went up and tried to do stand-up comedy. The problem was that he was sitting down! He kept telling up to not put our 40th anniversary Summit mugs in the dishwasher or they'd be wrecked. Regina then went back on rambling about how Peter Pan got Tinker Bell by clapping.

Finally, the projector worked. Within ten minutes into the slideshow, the DVD stopped. This happened twice and Tim then dismissed us early. I saw myself in the slideshow three times then the next day, I saw myself for the fourth time. Kevin found out from computer head, Troy, that he dropped the DVD accidently on a rock. Still, we went to bed and were excited about parent's day.

Day 25 was parent's day. It was very nice. My mom and all four of my grandparents came to see me. Since this was my maternal grandfather's first time at the camp, I gave a little tour to my family. My dad's parents had purchased me Genesis' *The Lamb Lies Down On Broadway* and meant to bring on parent's day. It didn't arrive so it would be sent out immediately once it came to their house. I had my mom also pre-order Alice Cooper's new album, which would come out on July 29th and I wouldn't be at a mall to purchase it. Still, I was given tons of junk food.

During the show on the horseshoe, someone walked onto our porch with his bags. It was Glenn. I was pleasantly shocked! Glenn was now back for second session but came early according to Neale. I was happy that Glenn was back. My dad's parents left and then my mom's parents waited for my mom to drop me off at the cabin to wait for Carl. I felt like crying but Carl prevented any tears.

Joel left around 3:30 pm for home. With that, there were eight of us. I decided to catch up and listen to my mall-bought albums on my iPod for the second time. Neale gave me the list of kids who would come second session. We didn't know any of them. It rained hard during horseshoe so Glenn played *Kung Pow* on his DVD player. I just wrote in my entry in my journal. I also learned that specialist Jon would be moving out of the cabin to make room for Jed of ST11. Tomorrow, he would be moving into our bunk. I wasn't happy with this. I wrote in my journal,

"Jed from ST11 is moving in soon while Jon is moving. Mark these words: Second session will be a nightmare."

This ends Session 1. If you wish to, you may go eat something or have some water. This took ten and a half pages so get ready for more. Here's Session 2.

At 4:00 am on Day 26, I was awoken by Summit Travel. Joe, Kevin, Seth, and Max were all leaving to have an early breakfast and head to the airport. I said goodbye to Max and everyone else. Once they left, I went to the bathroom. When I was in there, I felt as if I was going to cry. I had to stay strong so I went back to bed. When we awoke, there were only four of us: Aldan, Brandon, Glenn, and I. Carl would be the only counselor for this day as Simon was on his makeup day off and Carol had her day off but she stayed on camp because of her illness of Lyme's Disease. To help Carl, he had Nick of ST10 (also known as Phil since there was another Nick in ST10) to help out. They were so silly that morning for chores when they were singing and dancing to songs from musicals such as *The Lion King*, *Les Miserable*, and *Jesus Christ Superstar*. During "Circle Of Life", everyone acted out as all the animals. Neale came by, terrified by this. He did say two funny things. The first was,

"I did the right thing by not pairing you two up."

105

The second was,

"This is the most heterosexual bunk on camp."

We did have some of the normal period one for general swim, three for computers, rest hour boating, and six for AI. By sixth period, Jed was a member of ST12. I kept joking to Neale that we would need goats' blood and chicken feathers for a ritual to put Jed in our bunk! I think Jed found me a bit strange but I think he eventually got use to me. We also got our fourteenth perfect day of stars. By the end of the night, there were now five of us and other five were coming tomorrow.

Day 27 started off this morning. Carl had the day off and both Simon and Carol were in charge but Neale had to tell Carol to rest because of her illness. We were five until fourth period, when we were in the bunk watching *Spiderman*. Ernie arrived. We all shook hands and said hello. I'm not saying this to offend anyone but he was on the heavy side. Still, he seemed like a good guy.

During rest hour Jerry came by. He looked very social and was. I don't know why, but I felt I had a goal to be friends with him. During a free swim in the pool, Ruben came over. Tim was also there at rest hour and seemed very timid. He kind of reminded me of someone I knew!

We were now nine and after the first half of Walls and Ropes, we were ten. Liam came by. He was this skinny kid with glasses and we all said hello. Liam would be taking Max's bed, which was above my bed. However, Liam was really upset during dinner because I think his wisdom teeth were coming in. Jerry and Liam swapped beds as did Brandon and Garret the day before. Glenn took Joe's bed and Brandon took Seth's bed.

At the social that night, I had been speaking with Carol that this bunk is different but we can do great things still. Deep down inside, I felt as if that wasn't true.

Day 28 was our first trip day of the session. We were to have our Round Robin but due to the rain, we had another lame Bingo game. Our BBQ lunch was indoors and soon after, we went to the movie theaters. I knew I'd have a lot of money because of the $70 I got from my family on parents day. Adding up the money I had before, the money I earned from work periods in Newspaper and Computers, and the $12 "welcoming" gift I had a total of $129!

I just got a milkshake and cookie. Glenn and I then went to the theater and saw *The Dark Knight*. It was really good although it was hard to understand at times. Little did we know outside of camp, critics were praising the movie and the late Heath Ledger's performance as the Joker.

We then went to the Viewmont Mall. I was in a group with Carl, Tim, Jed, and Ernie. I went to FYE and blew some bucks on five albums. They were The Band's *The Band*, Judas Priest's *Unleashed In The East* and *Defenders Of The Faith*, Motley Crue's *Dr. Feelgood*, and the Ramones' *Rocket To Russia*. In fact, *Defenders Of The Faith* was free since I got it with the other Judas Priest album in the "Buy 1, Get 1" bin. Carl and Steve kept singing on the ride back while throughout the day, Tim tried to talk to me. I didn't know yet that he felt left out.

Day 29 got me pissed off when we just got all but a few stars. We went in a steamed pool, tennis, and music. At music, we all sang karaoke and I sang "Smoke on the Water". We were all laughing when Glenn and Carol sang "Summer Nights". We were laughing as we had never heard of the song before.

Towards the end of discovery during fifth period, I was asked by Sandra to give an opinion or something on what we were doing. I had nothing to say. Everyone else was a little crazy because we were touching the toxic stuff in diapers. Aldan then said used a big word to describe me and I can't remember what it was. Whatever it was, the word meant "without emotion". I walked off immediately and had to speak with Carl when we got back to the cabin. I told him once again that Aldan better watch his mouth. Carl said he spoke with him and he said he was sorry.

Next, we had Tribes with Julie. Ruben also gave some members of the bunk these trances. I would record them and they were fun to watch, especially Glenn's. We also had another Acid Trip night, or Talent Night rather. I also had written a letter in my black journal to Carl, Simon, and Carol about my worries for this new version of ST12. Carl read it that night and found it mature.

Day 30 saw a perfect day of stars. We had to enjoy it because we didn't have many perfect days that session. I described the day in my journal as weird. We hiked across the road and that was so cool. Computers was next and then we had to waiter. During this time and into rest hour, we were informed that Tim was moving to ST5 because Neale and my counselors thought he'd be happier there. We were always active and Tim just wasn't like us.

We had our laundry period then a funny video arts, in which we went in front of the green screen. The majority of the bunk wanted to do a spoof on the video game *Halo*. I was reluctant at first but I went up there twice. The second time I was to random. My scene was with Aldan and we were to be talking about the mission. I started off by saying that the ship looked nice and that we got it from Sears. The funniest bit was when Aldan said,

108

"I'm not feeling good about this alien attack…"

"You know what I do when I see an alien?" I said.

"What?"

"I just take the sharpest object and go 'meeooww!'"

Almost everybody was laughing! We had canteen that night and it was also International Night. This show had all the counselors and specialists up on the stage for their country. They'd do a dance or sing something related to that country. Simon and Jon went up for England. Simon was David Beckham while Jon was Charlie Chaplin. Jon wasn't living with us but he was still our specialist. However with Tim's departure, there was now a chance he'd come back.

Day 31 was an almost perfect day of stars. In the middle of the night, Liam woke us up. What I remember was hearing him yell,

"Somebody help me! Somebody help me!"

Most of the guys were saying "Shut the fuck up, Liam" or "What the hell?" It turned out he was having a bad dream. I went to my work period for computers instead of home economics, where they made apple crumble. We were doing fine up until soccer, where we were given three and a half stars.

Go-Karts was canceled so we had early showers. The social was funny because when I was talking with Carl, I spotted Tim and Regina. Carl then joked around and told me he had to look busy. So, I had to fake a cry out! I also went up with Brandon to get snacks for the bunk at night.

Meanwhile, ST11 were talking to Jed about if he did anything with his girlfriend. He said he didn't do anything. I then told them about a couple there and that Mama C spotted out some kissing action. Sooner or later, Jed came into the bunk pissed at me and said,

"Thanks a lot, Aaron."

What did I do? Apparently, he thought I was referring to him as the kissing action. I told him I was talking about another couple, not him. Carl went outside to talk with him and I even offered him that we could go to Friendly's and forget about it. Carl came back out later and said that Jed wasn't angry at me. His anger was directed at me. I was fine with this and we went to sleep.

Day 32 wasn't good from what I remember. The morning was fine, according to my journal. During general swim, I got a little depressed. It was most likely because I was the only person in the bunk who didn't play any trading card game. I felt so alone without Max. I even admitted that I didn't have a friend. What about Jerry? He was already pissing everybody off and he got me pissed off when we were at Walls and Ropes. We were at this station where a person had to fall back while the rest of the bunk had to catch the person. We had to be serious about this and have nice long arms out. Jerry was saying I wasn't doing it right and after three times I just said,

"If you're going to keep perfecting me, then forget it!"

Also, the bunk was getting girl crazy. Jerry, Liam, Aldan, and Jed all had girlfriends. It was crazy. Actually, Jerry and Liam were on the search for some meat. I love being sarcastic! That night was a very lame *Night At The Museum* night. I just listened to music and wrote in my black journal.

Day 33 was another hell-on-earth day for me. The morning was kind of annoying me. Everyone was obsessing over "the game". See, I just lost. It was something that was stupid and anytime someone mentioned about the game, everyone loses. When we were in textiles, almost everyone was making a shirt that said something about the game. I didn't because Uriah Heep meant more to me!

I got to catch up in getting pictures from the camp's website early for the slideshow I make after the year is over. After clubs ended that night, a girl from GST6 came to me and said there was someone in her bunk that liked me. Glenn was telling me this during showers also. The girl asked me if I would talk to her. I responded by saying I'd think about it. I know that the average male would think this was a good thing.

For me, I didn't know what to say. I really only had the bunk to talk to and when I told them that I don't date yet, they started to think I had some kind of illness or something. The reason why I don't date for now is because I don't have enough friends back at home. Also, this was camp. I wrote "Kosher Kisses" as a joke to how stupid the dating is and this would've been hypocritical for me. Luckily, nothing happened and I'm happy with my choice.

Day 34 was a day of perfect stars but not everyone was happy. The morning was good and we even had a free swim during swim instruction due to lack of staff. Lunch that day for me was weird because my table was having a cook out without telling Neale or anybody. I had no choice but to take everything that I spent so much time setting up. I was going to speak with Julie during fifth period but that period was choice and I didn't know where she would be. I then asked Carol and she got angry at me for not sitting down. So I didn't get to go to computers and was forced to go to Arts and Crafts.

I later apologized to Carol at general swim and she said it was alright. We had baseball canceled and had early showers. While walking around during horseshoe, I bumped into counselor James from ST11. He invited me to the Nintendo Hut along with some of the other campers from ST11. James was a great guy. He's from Scotland and he was very funny and very kind. It would've been cool if I had him as a counselor with Carl, Simon, and Carol but that would never happen!

After horseshoe, I got back to the cabin and told Simon and Carol where I was. We knew what the evening activity was going to be. It would be a meeting about the rules from tomorrow's trip day at Hershey Park. Before we left for the dining hall, Ernie was hitting himself with a Croc sandal. He was doing it so much that I asked Simon what he was trying to do.

"He's trying to get attention." answered Simon

I thought it was getting annoying and I went in the cabin and blared music.

Day 35 was our big trip to Hershey Park. We rode in a coach bus, which was great compared to the school buses we had for Dorney Park. It turned out Carol couldn't come because of her illness with Lyme's Disease. I was in a group with Glenn, Liam, and a counselor named Katie. She had arrived to camp just a week or so ago. She would be teaching periods for campers to create sculptures. She seemed very nice and we had a great time.

The only things we did were going on a blue train, see a sea lion show, go to the zoo, go on the merry-go-round, and go to the arcade. Glenn was so funny with his $200 at the arcade. He kept playing the *Deal Or No Deal* game there. He ended up giving me the tickets he earned since he couldn't stand Liam, which was nice of him.

We did go to a store where they sold rock merchandise. I was looking thru the t-shirts and found a really cool one with John Lennon on it. It was him standing with his arms crossed and wearing a shirt that said "New York City", where the picture was taken. The picture, taken by photographer Bob Gruen, I had seen a lot in black & white but this was a painting of that picture and the artist added color to it. I wanted to buy it but all I saw were extra large sizes. Katie was looking through random shirts and managed to find one in large. I decided to buy it and I love wearing it.

We went to Chocolate World in the end. I got to see the tour with Carl and Simon. They were too funny during the tour. I bought some Hershey bars, including a pack with six bars. Also, Glenn and I thought of Carol during the trip. Our group decided to buy her a gift that wasn't chocolate since she hated Hershey's. We got her a mug with her name on it. When we got back at 10:15 pm that night, she liked it very much and used it during the rest of the year.

Day 36 was easy from what I wrote. With a work period in the morning, I had general swim only. During a bunk period in third period, I was finally able to talk with Julie. I talked about my fears of not having any friends this session. We didn't get enough time to talk so Julie said that we should talk tomorrow. Music was next and then we had our rest hour.

When the music started to play for fifth period, Carol fainted. I didn't see it happen but when it did everybody inside ran outside to tell us. Dr. Steve and his team came to the cabin to check Carol while we went to Discovery and did an egg drop experiment.

During our early showers, I got two packages in the mail. They were both of the albums I was waiting on. Those albums were Alice Cooper's newest album *Along Came a Spider* and Genesis' *The Lamb Lies Down On Broadway*. I was very happy and very spoiled! I immediately listen to Alice and decided to listen to my Genesis album the next day since it was a double concept album! We had our talent night but this was the problem: Carl was deputing, Carol was sick, and Simon had the night off. Jon, who moved back in on Day 34, and Jen from adventure were in charge of us that night.

Day 37 was a day of perfect stars. Still, not everyone was happy. I started my day with newspaper and then camp crafts. I was able to get both of my new albums onto my iPod at computers, which meant I could listen to the Genesis album on there! I listened to the first disc during rest hour.

During this time, Ernie was once again trying to get attention. He had made a sword at one period using a wooden stick and some aluminum foil. He took the foil off and then started to bang the stick into the wall near is bed. Everyone was pissed and when he was told to stop, he kept doing it. It got so bad that Neale had to come in and kick us out of the cabin for a while.

Video Arts was just a period of watching a documentary about the world that was made by the BBC. I got a break from doing the laundry during our early showers from Carl, telling him I had done it for three or four weeks in a row and I had a long album to continue. He agreed and I continued listening to my Genesis album. We also got our chocolate, which was so good. That night was the second session Camper-Counselor night. It wasn't that good since I wasn't in it!

Day 38 was just pure madness. We had to waiter in the morning and from time to time, it was raining that day. We also had a crazy cleanup period, in which both ST11 and ST12 had a war, by taking each other's stuff. I wasn't really a part of this. We had all normal periods for the morning but after nature, it rained. Using the TV with a DVD play that we stole from ST11, I popped in *The Naked Gun* and then Simon put in the sequel.

When we were finished watching the sequel, which was the end of horseshoe, we were told by Ruben and Glenn to all sit on our beds. Once this was done, Glenn and Ruben both said that we would have a discussion on what we would approve on for the rest of the year. Glenn was pretty much in charge.

This discussion was making me angry in a way. One thing was that I was upset that we were having this conversation in the first place. Also, I thought the counselors had picked Ruben and Glenn. Ruben is younger than me and I'd love to be a leader one of these days. When it came to me on what I should approve on, I said I was great on getting myself down. When Glenn dismissed us, he picked me last to tell me I should work on socializing. I just wanted to get the sharpest object and throw it anywhere because I *was* working on this already! However, Glenn didn't know and he was off the hook.

So I was both angry and jealous, and I told this to Carl. That seemed to help and so did Simon, who finally helped me, shave my uni-brow. I also found out that we would be the white team for Track And Field day. The curse continued with me being on the team that won the year before.

Day 39 was an awkward day. We had every period, starting with basketball. During rest hour, we watched *Red vs. Blue*, which was this silly show with *Halo* shots.

I did the Leap of Faith during Walls and Ropes. What is the Leap of Faith? It's when after you climb something; you stand on this platform with a rope and everything to keep you safe. Then, you had to just jump off and try ringing the cowbell that was up there. After this, you were lowered down. This was my first time doing this since 2005.

After horseshoe, we all had to sit on our beds again to know that the "war" between ST11 and ST12 was over. Brandon had tried to resolve it with a peace treaty but ST11 just ripped it up. Since this didn't work, Brandon silly-stringed ST11's cabin inside and on the outside. Brandon was refusing to clean it up, which was really weird because Brandon is a really nice guy. We then went to movie night, were they watched *21*. I spoke with Julie in the SIT trailer during this time.

Day 40 was Track And Field Day. We were the white team. We went from station to station, trying to use teamwork and all. I kept joking to Neale that we were the "Caucasian team" since there was one day when he said he teams were red, Caucasian, and blue! Jed and Jerry were fighting every period.

During the last period, which was running, I didn't want to run and had people take my place. Jerry pointed out towards the end that I hadn't done shit and that I was a "lazy hippy". The other members of the bunk, for the one and only time, agreed with Jerry. Jed threw in that he was fucking pissed with me.

When it came to Brandon, he had no problem. I told Carl that everyone wanted to kill me. In short, Jerry apologized soon after. At the end of the day, white came in second place while blue won the whole thing.

Day 41 was a perfect day of stars but it wasn't easy. Since we were tired from the day before, we took Drama off. We then had all of the normal periods except baseball, which was canceled. To my surprise, everyone in the bunk watched *The Naked Gun 33 1/3*. We did also get to go to the Wii Hut during choice period. The evening activity was a secret from us. We were just told to go to the AI field. Once we got there, we saw boxes of pizza, chips, soda, and cake. I knew what this was: it was the party that all the bunks put money into. It was fun but for some, it was sad. I was just lying down on a mat we had to sit on and looking at the sky. I don't why I did that!

Day 42 was our last trip day. We first had our morning clubs. I had computers then practice with Carl for the dance we would be doing for the ST/GST play of *High School Musical*. Ruben, Jed, and I with other guys would be dancing to the song "Bop to the Top". We then had our BBQ.

We then went to the Wayne County Fair. I was in a group with Simon, Glenn, and Liam. We went to see the hog races, which was too funny. Simon decided to kiss one of the pigs. What he had to do was take a cookie and put it in his mouth. The pig would then take it out of his mouth. It was too funny and Carl and Neale were there to see it also. Simon was really funny. For the entire year, he kept me laughing and was also very caring too.

Next, we went to the Steamtown Mall for dinner and some shopping. I was only told last night that we were going to the mall. Had I known before, I wouldn't have spent the money I did at Hershey Park (except keep the Lennon shirt). Still, I got three albums. They were Bob Dylan's *Bringing It All Back Home*, Judas Priest's *Hell Bent for Leather*, and Lou Reed's *Berlin*.

I thought I wouldn't have the money but I noticed when the clerk scanned the Judas Priest album, the machine said it cost $.00. I asked if that one was free. He said yes it was and it was apart of their "Buy two, get one free" deal. I was pleasantly shocked. On the way back to camp, I listened to the Judas Priest album and then back in the cabin, I listened to the Bob Dylan album.

Day 43 was fine. We started that day with general swim. I then had a work period in computers then tennis. During a game, Jerry started to get pissed that I was sucking at the game. Carl tried to tell me to do my best and I did but Jerry still wasn't happy. With that I just said,

"You know what, fuck it."

I threw the tennis racket on the ground and Carl told me in a calm voice to sit down and he'd talk to me. I think when we came to me, I apologized for my outburst and Carl said something like we all get angry and Jerry did apologize.

Music was good for the most part while rest hour was dance practice. In discovery, we made stress balls. During my work period at newspaper, I broke mine and Sandra helped me make another one quickly. That one broke the next day. It was this dough in a balloon! When the bunk watched the rest of *21*, I was forced to go outside and listen to the Lou Reed album. That day was also Jon's 25th birthday. For a shocker, talent night wasn't that bad.

Day 44 would a stressful one and none of us were ready for it. We started with mountain biking despite some rain. During second, we had play practice for second and third period. We then waitered but when we were at general swim during rest hour, thunder sounded with the sun still out. The period was immediately canceled and we went back into the cabin.

We were told by our counselors to sit on our beds. Everybody was in except Jerry. Carl then told us that the reason why we were having this meeting is because everybody was bullying Jerry. The counselors didn't like it at all and Carl said we must raise our hand to speak. I was, once again, innocent pretty much. The only thing I told the bunk was if you have nothing good to say about somebody, then it is best if you keep your mouth shut.

Everyone else said that it wasn't their fault but Jerry's fault. Everyone felt as if the counselors were taking sides, which they were not doing at all. Carl, Simon, and Carol all said if they had a problem, go on Regina's porch. Everyone started to argue and then I said that if anyone was doing anything to anyone, then stop it. Glenn, of all people, then says I was acting so innocent when I'm not.

"Boo-Hoo, I miss the first session. I know, I'll just keep to myself" Glenn said trying to mock me. "What do you do? Talk to Carl?"

"Don't you just play with your recorder?" asked Jed.

That's when I just got up and said "Fuck all of you" and flipped them off at the same time. I stormed out the door and plopped myself on the bench on the porch were Carl and Carol were speaking to Jerry. Carl pointed out that this was rude and I knew that. Carol pulled me aside and I told her what happened.

While I was trying to talk to her during interruptions, I started to cry. Carol put her arm around me and said that the bunk was immature not to take my lead. She then suggested I go in the cabin to hear what Neale had to say.

When Neale started speaking, I just put a *Survivor* buff around my eyes and cried. By the time it was our laundry period and

119

the AI staff arrived, only three boys were in the cabin. They were Jerry, Ernie, and I. We just relaxed and then went to Video Arts, where we just played with clay.

Before horseshoe, everyone had to apologize for something and then they could go out and have horseshoe time. I apologized to Carol about interrupting the conversation she and Carl were having with Jerry. I had nothing to apologize to Simon about and he said so himself. I was waiting for two apologies and would not leave until I heard them. Jed said sorry but Glenn felt that he didn't need to. Despite this, the *High School Musical* play went great. We had treats afterwards which included real ice cream!

Day 45 was hard day. I couldn't waiter for breakfast after complaining of pain in my "man-bits", as Simon likes to say it. Everything else was so good that we even had a bunk movie with the third *Matrix*, which I didn't watch. This was until sixth period when I had a pain in my teeth. It felt like my wisdom teeth were coming in. I kept crying about it afterwards.

Sixth period, which was soccer didn't go very well. There was fighting and we sat at Go-Karts with Carol to talk about it. Once again, I was innocent and when Glenn came back from work, Carol told him to go back to the bunk. I asked if I could to since I was innocent and Carol let me go. I went to the medical center with Carl after dinner to have my teeth checked out. For that day and the next, I was given this pain numbing stuff. I didn't have the pain ever since.

Glenn also apologized about the day before and that night, we had the option of swimming or social. I chose to swim. Sadly that day, we learned that Bernie Mac had passed away. Another person, who cheered me up after my dad's passing, was now gone.

Day 46 was pretty crazy. Carl and Carol told us that last night, a bear was on the horseshoe and was actually behind the cabin of ST12 at midnight. We were scared but we all lived! The only period we had that morning was ceramics. Otherwise, we were in the Wii Hut and in the cabin. General swim was canceled but we still had games in the dining room with the waterfront staff. For the next two periods, we were in the cabin watching *Ace Ventura* as a reward. It was too funny!

We also saw the unit plays of *Annie* and *Scooby Doo*. They were alright. In fact, it was so funny that one of the plays was *Scooby Doo*. During the night of Day 25, Carl was on duty and James came to the cabin and said to Carl,

"You want to come with me? I'm watching *Scooby Doo 2*."

Carl immediately started laughing because of the way James said the movie's title. Carl kept saying it the next day and it became a reoccurring joke!

Day 47 saw more rain. We also saw the last two plays, *Peter Pan* and *Beetlejuice*. Both were alright. Before our early lunch, the bunk found another mouse and Brandon carried it out with his hands. We had every period in the afternoon including boating during rest hour, arts and crafts, and AI.

That day saw me trying to pack my carry-on. Before Horseshoe was called, it started to rain hard. It took Tim a long time to decide that we would have a "walking" horseshoe. James of ST11 took a few of us down to computers for only ten minutes. In those ten minutes, I found out that Isaac Hayes had passed away the day before. Ironically enough, he and Bernie Mac were to be in a movie together called *Soul Men*, with Hayes as a supporting actor. That night was also our lame ass prom.

Day 48 marked two days of perfect stars but it didn't matter. We had normal periods, including our last time waitering. During this, I came up with the idea that we should all tear off our aprons and run slowly at the samee time and all yell,

"Freedom!"

I tried telling Simon and Carol to spread the word around about this. I tried telling a few people from our bunk also and only six people listened to leave their aprons on. Once Tim called for first bunk ready to go, we ran and did it! It was too funny.

Simon told us to all sit outside the bunk and wait. When we got inside, there was soda and candy. We were also allowed to eat our own food, I think. It was pretty cool. For the annual banquet that night, I had my hair combed nice and my Rolling Stones *Some Girls* vest on with jeans. People were saying I was looking sharp and even Neale say so too. It's a banquet, right?

That night was also the longest announcements when campers and counselors got rewarded. I got a jacket for my five years at the camp. The only problem was that when Mayer read off the names, he pronounced my last name as "cone"! Carl also got a jacket for his four years at the camp. We also saw the staff play of *Cinderella*, which was alright.

Day 49 would've been a trip day but since this was our last full day, we stayed at camp. We had Round Robin at morning, which is a smaller version of Track And Field Day. Last year, Neale's unit won as the black team. Neale wanted us to be the black team again. I had Alice Cooper make up on and even danced to the anthems of the camp. We ended up winning but there was no prize. I was so pissed but it made sense since it was the last full day.

We had our BBQ and were able to pack up. We were then forced to watch *Into The Blue* during fifth period. I didn't watch and listened to Frank Zappa. We had early showers and a regular horseshoe. That night we saw the second session slideshow, which I was in four times.

Then at the waterfront, I began to cry so much. I couldn't stop. I had to hug so many people. Carol hugged me and said that hopefully we'll be in the same unit next year. It was such a sad night as they always light the year and this glow-stick dance to the song "Aquarius" by the band Aqua. Even back in the cabin, Ernie was so negative and started to sing "All You Need Is Love" but replaced 'love' with 'hate'.

Day 50 was the last day logically. We had our breakfast and then went back to the cabin. Aldan, Jed, and Liam all left for their plane. The bus for Philadelphia wasn't a long wait and my counselors walked me down. I gave everyone a hug. When Carl hugged me, he told me to stay positive. I held my tears back and went on the bus. When I did eventually see my mom, I started to cry. What a long strange trip, man!

Since camp has ended, I haven't been doing much. As I finished this in August, I don't have much to say for now in this first draft. I've only had contact with Glenn and Max. Max apologized that session two was bad! As for next year, I'm planning on going for my sixth year in 2009. As I will be 17 years old next summer, this will be my last year. I'm thinking about looking into becoming a counselor when I turn 18 years old for the summer of 2010.

Although that place called college is calling my name, I'm trying not to think so much about the future. I would like to look at my fifth year as a mature then immature year. I had my favorite counselor with me and my favorite unit leader with me again, both for the third time. I had two other great counselors and made some strong friendships in a way. It was a hell of a ride.

THE END!

Aftermath
March 31, 2009- Former Summit Camp head counselor, Tim Kedge, dies at his home after being sick for some couple months. It's on April 2 when camp families are alerted on the news. Nobody knows how he died but one thing is for sure: the world had just lost a great man and his name was Tim Kedge.

Tim Kedge: A Wise Man (1949-2009)

Tim Kedge
1949-2009

There was never a day at camp when Tim didn't do the announcements. I remember how loud it was on that first day in 2004. I had never seen so many people loud and excited about announcements. I later saw that the ring leader of all this was this old man with grey hair and round glasses. He was English and will probably be the only English man I've ever heard use the word "folks". As I went to camp for five summers, I have plenty of memories of Tim. I can remember in 2006 when it was the end of the year. Tim always announced services the camp was having. That night was for Catholic Services. Tim had the tendency to stutter so I remember him saying,

"Those of who wish to attend the Catholic…Catholic services…"

My bunk had a laugh as we thought the services were now twice as Catholic. I can also remember one night in 2007, we were on the AI field for our evening activity. Tim rarely gives announcements after Horseshoe but on this night, he did. I remember my bunk wasn't feeling great as we were arguing a little. Then out of nowhere, Tim comes on the speakers and says,

"Hi there, folks. Uh, I would like to know if there's anyone here on camp who happens to have a *puussh* pin. Yes, a *push* pin. If you can help, that would be great."

We all burst into laughter because it was so random. In 2008, I was lucky enough to interview Tim for the camp's paper as I was writing an article on the camp's 40th summer. I had to speak to Tim so I could get through Mayer. I let Tim know that some of my questions were for him. When I was introduced to Tim, he shook my hand and thought it was wonderful that I was writing about Summit. When I asked Tim when he first came to camp, he just stared at the ceiling.

"The camp's site says you came as counselor in 1978" I said.

"That might be right" Tim said as he lowered his head down. "Those were the days when I was a young man!"

We both laughed as did the other person who was in his office. I seriously looked up to Tim as an announcer. If you read my essays or anything I write, there's a little bit of Tim in each of them.

126

I don't know where but it's in there. During the summer of 2009, there were a couple of other changes. Tim didn't get to see these changes but I think he's proud that Summit is carrying on where he left off.

Rest in peace, Tim

Peace and love,

Aaron Conn
January 17, 2010

The Camp: Season 6
By Aaron Conn

There was a time when I said that I'd never do sleep-away camp. I ended up doing just that in 2004 and nothing was really stopping after 2008, despite a rather unpleasant second session. At that time, I said that I wouldn't want to do Summit's traveling program. I did in 2009. This year was different from the others and had me in places I'd never been to. This is my sixth year with Summit!

Preface

Do I need to say whether this is necessary? It is. I actually came back home after my 2008 year anxious. I had no idea what would come next. Still, I entered into my junior year at school. I really tried to stick out that year and I think I did so. I was supporting two local bands related to my school. I felt I was a human being and socializing with people. I didn't get to interview any big names in music though.

I tried not to think about camp until January. By then, things weren't sounding so great. The camp's head counselor and announcer, Tim Kedge, was said to be sick around the holidays in 2008. A few months later it was announced that Robbie G, who's known for giving out bunk stars, would take Tim's job. At the same time they announced this, the camp said Tim was at home recovering. This left me puzzled.

I tried keeping in contact with counselors, such as Carl. He had emailed me and said that he would be doing travel for both trips. I was signed on to do a full session for camp so that was the end of my stay with Carl. I was aware that Simon and Carol would return but camper wise, I didn't know.

On April 2 2009, Max called me to tell me the news that everyone had already known: Tim Kedge had passed away on March 31, 2009. I was shocked but at the same time not. Max then spilled more salt in my wounds and told me he was only doing the travel program for the first trip.

I hung up soon after and just cried. My life was moving along but then Tim dies and Max isn't going back to camp. I was also aware that the directors for travel would be former unit leaders (and married) Pete and Dannelle. If anyone recalls, Dannelle was my first unit leader. I had some thinking to do.

It didn't take me long to make a choice. I asked for a list of kids already signed up for both camp and travel. In the camp list I saw names like Seth, Jed, Liam, Ruben, and even Tim. On the travel list, I saw familiar names. Also I knew that Carl would be there. I made up my mind: I was doing travel.

For the months that followed, I kept in contact with anyone I could and created both a Facebook account and group for Travel 2009. A few days before the trip started, I got to speak with Dannelle. It was good to hear her voice after a long time.

Dannelle told me I'd be with Max (which I already knew) and my group counselors were named Gary and Dawson. A few minutes later, Dawson called and I spoke with him. He sounded nice and had read my letter. I was excited.

It was June 23, 2009 that my mom and I had to leave. The trip would start the next day but we were all to meet at the airport in Newark, New Jersey. My mom and I stayed overnight at her aunt and uncle's house. So on June 24, my mom and I got to the airport. I had my carry-on and my suitcase. We kept walking on and on, trying to find Summit. When we found them, I spotted Carl but he couldn't see me. I just got in his corner and said his name. He looked and gave me a hug. Max was there and we just smiled.

My mom and I then met Gary and Dawson. My mom got to talk with Gary and found out he was 50 years old. Mama C, who had been in Neale's unit as long as Carl had, was there too as a floater (which meant she had no group of the four). After we said our goodbyes to our families, we got in our groups. The Gary-Dawson group consisted of Max, CJ, Joe, Joseph, Eli, Seth, Otto, and Byron. We were the only group that had no girls.

After Pete's introduction, we went through security and then a suite already waiting for us. We had lunch. I was with Max the whole time. I wanted to know other people for sure but for now, I was with Max. We got on the plane around noon to Denver, Colorado. I sat with counselor Tim and a camper named Sierra.

When we landed, we took a crazy trip to baggage claim and met up with our coach bus for the trip. Our driver's name was Roger and he'd be with us for the whole trip. We would meet Dannelle in Utah as she was still teaching. We departed for our first lodging, which was a Best Western.

Although we were told rooming would be mixed, that didn't stop Max and me as we had planned months before to room. Still, we had a third roommate and that was Otto. From what I hear, Otto has Tourette's so he'd be off in his own world. I can't help but relate him to Alec from my first two years and Patrick from the next two. For the whole time, it felt like there were only two people. We just kept an eye on Otto, especially me.

When we got in the room, I couldn't believe my eyes. What stood before me was what a camper at Summit would crave for: comfortable beds, a clean bathroom, and a television. I got to hook

130

up the TV to my new portable DVD player. I'm going to say this for the record: this player survived the entire trip and is a lot better than the one I had for 2005.

Around 7 or 8 at night, we went down to the small breakfast area and had pizza from Blackjack's. Pete also had us in a quick meeting. We had to give our phones and cameras (although that changed after four days), which was no problem for me. Max and I watched *Pink Floyd: Live In Pompeii* and got to bed at 11.

Day 2 was nice at the beginning. We had a crazy continental breakfast and then had the bus take us to Elich Gardens, an amusement park. We stuck in our groups. I didn't go on any rides in the park but soon we got to the water park. We all got to go in the lazy river but soon after, it started to really rain.

The water park closed so we were left in doors and forced into browsing at the gift shops. We did get to go back to the water park and I got to talk with Gary when I was doing nothing. Carl and I were going to do the wave pool but the life guard wanted us out. This halted plans for dinner and we were left clueless.

Pete had us go on the bus and we went to Walmart since people had to get some things. I didn't need anything but I bought a cheap copy of Aerosmith's *Live Bootleg*. We got back to the hotel and chilled in our rooms for the time being.

I had the TV on and flipped CNN on. I thought I had heard some crazy story on the bus and heard the same thing between two Walmart cashiers. The news sounded so bogus that I just checked. I found out then that what I had heard wasn't a lie: Michael Jackson had suddenly passed away from cardiac arrest earlier in the day. He was 50 years old.

As a music journalist and just happened to respect and like his music, it was a **huge** shock for me (so huge that I didn't know that Farrah Fawcett had also died that day. I found out the next day). I almost felt like crying. Max was a bit shocked but I was so shocked that my heart raced. As a group, we walked in the rain to a Red Robin. We were all talking about the sad news and music in general. It was nice just to hang out as a group. Max and I watched a Frank Zappa DVD and went to bed.

Day 3 was our last day in our first Best Western hotel. Still, Gary had Max and I help with a picnic lunch. We filled a water jug with powder Gatorade and bathtub water. I had to use my arm to mix the powder.

As soon as we got our suitcase and bags on the bus, we were off to Cave of the Winds. We split into different groups and went into this long cave. It was really nice. The next thing we did was seeing some of the mountains in Denver. We had a tour guide on the bus and it was nice. There were a few stops when we could get out and take pictures.

After a nice long day, we got to the University of Colorado. It took us a while to get in our dorms but Max and I had one room while CJ, Joe, and Joseph had the other. The dorms were awful. The beds were like concrete. After dinner, it was difficult to put up with CJ, Joe, and Joseph. They were basically off the wall and going nuts. It was everything from dirty humor to whatever. Although I am still friends with all three now, it was hard then.

I was so stressed that I told Max for tonight while we were in the rec center, I would go swimming. I also told Dawson this and he let me use his towel. It was really nice and Carl was there too. I went on the slide they had. Still, Max and I had to put up with the noise outside us that night.

I woke up on Day 4 all warm and sick. I could get out of bed and I tried telling Gary. At breakfast, I made sure I ate a lot and that seemed to work. Soon enough, I was better. My guess to why I was sick would probably be from the mold in the room.
Anyway, we went to the Olympic Center.

Next, we went to the mall. We also had the chance to see a movie. First, we had lunch. Next, Max and I did a little shopping. We stopped at Borders. I bought two albums by Yes, *Fragile* and *Close to the Edge*. I used my debit card because we were in a hurry to get to our movie (*Star Trek*, my second time seeing it). We all got debit cards with $300 on them from our parents. Since I would be going on both trips, I had $600.

The cashier liked my purchases and went on and on about how great the albums were. I was just thinking "Shut up! We got a movie to see!" Luckily, Max and I made it for *Star Trek*. Max liked it despite not understanding it.

After the movie, Max and I stopped by a closing K Mart. I bought Edgar Winter's *They Only Come at Night*, Hals, and some Febreze. It felt weird getting the latter because it's something I don't buy normally! It was for the filthily dorms. Next, we went to the Flying W Ranch. There, we went on these mountains and looked at all the shops they had there.

Our dinner was supposed to be outside but when it started raining, we went indoors. They called us by table to get our dinner. It wasn't that good. After that there was a live band they had playing was pretty good and funny. Everyone had a laugh when they performed "I Am My Own Grandpa", which is a song that I remembered from *The Muppet Show*. As for the night, it was like the one before it.

We woke up pretty late on Day 5 and we were told why: we weren't going anywhere today and stayed on campus all day. Dawson and Carl brought us some pancakes and eggs from Denny's. We hung in our rooms and I listened to the rest of my music.

Lunch was Blackjacks and sooner or later, we heard there was a warning for a tornado. With that, the counselors had us all moved to one hallway. We were told to bring nothing but I saw people with iPods and all. I sat in the back where there was no campers.

Mama C spotted me and sat down. When she asked me what was wrong, I told her that I was a bit stressed not knowing who's telling the truth. She then spoke on her walkie-talkie and within minutes, we had a meeting. The good news was that we were safe from any tornado. The bad news was that we would be staying another night.

The reason why we didn't do anything today was because a camper named was sick with symptoms of the flu. From the medical terms, it sounded like swine flu (which there was an outbreak of in May earlier that year) but just to be safe, Dr. Steve back at camp and some other big heads said to stay on campus for today.

As for dinner, the college had made us sandwiches. Gary had Max, CJ, and I all help push the carts with the bags on there. We got to wear surgical masks, which was fun for me. I had my hat on with my sunglasses on and then this mask. I then started imitating Rorschach from *Watchmen*, which was funny and Gary picked up on it. The lunch was terrible but both Gary and Dawson allowed Max and I to bring it down to our rooms. We got early showers and watched *Almost Famous* on my DVD player. Max hadn't seen it before and enjoyed it.

Day 6 had us eating breakfast in a different area as we were under self-quarantine. This day was an improvement as we actually had activities planned out. Pete pulled me aside and asked me if I'd help Tim write the newsletter for travel. I helped a little but it was nice and different.

At lunch, I let Carl know that it had been three years since ST6 (in short, three years since I met Carl and Max). After lunch, there was an option to take part in water gun activities. Max and I watched *The Godfather* instead. They sounded like they were having fun and maybe too much fun.

On our way to dinner, I had to escort Carl because he was afraid someone would go at him. Max and I listened to music and in a group meeting, we found out we were staying another day at the university. Still, Carl stopped by our room and said hello to Max and I.

Day 7 was nice from the start. We got to swim in the pool and have lunch. After being in our dorms much too long, we went to rec center and played in the basketball area. I just dribbled a ball. For dinner, the counselors went out and got us McDonald's. Max and I decided to watch the *Wingspan* documentary by Paul McCartney but we were all called up to the main room.

We were all force to watch *Fantastic Four,* which was all camper Aden's idea. No one liked it. They were texting and crap. It got so loud that counselor Ted (who is a great guy with his thick southern/Virginian accent) yelled,

"Everybody hush up and watch the movie!"

Everyone laughed but stayed quiet but it didn't help too much. I made a point to counselor Beth that there were some of us that wanted to be in our dorms. Beth allowed us to do so and with that, Max and I went back watching our documentary.

In short, we were called up once again and we were all told that we were staying *another* night. I was crying a bit when Dawson came by to check up on us.

Day 8 started out simple. Max and I watched *This Is Spinal Tap*. While our movie played, CJ went mad and pissed in the shower and bathroom floor. I was disgusted. Still, we got to go outside and I walked in a group with Carl. I told him about my idea of making a concept album on travel. He liked it told me to tell someone else. This was Carl's way of saying he knew all my tricks, I guess.

After lunch, the counselors were taking names for people who wanted to go to the doctor's. Max had a bit of a fever the last time we were all checked (we were checked for the past few days and nights) and with Seth and Dawson; they went to the doctor's. The rest of us went to the Air Force. We were now allowed to get out and we'd found out on that day that tomorrow we would be out of the University of Colorado. So it was nice to get out the goddamned place.

When we came back for dinner, I saw Max. He was fine but the people who had gone to the doctor's had to go to the hospital. I just waited in the room, listening to Wings, and at 9pm we went to Walmart. As for groups, I kept an eye on Otto. I bought Heaven & Hell's (better known as Black Sabbath without Ozzy Osbourne) *The Devil You Know* and Bob Dylan's *Together Through Life*. Gary then questioned me (it wasn't the first time) on buying everyday items such as CDs.

I took it a little too seriously and said I wouldn't buy any music unless I can't get it back home. For the record, I kept to that for the rest of the trip but I would buy more music for sure. My mom told me to tell Gary I had a habit.

Anyway, we got back at 10 and I took a late shower. Gary told me that he had made CJ clean the bathroom earlier that day. Max returned later. He and the other three guys were talking. I kept hearing that the trip would be canceled and shit like that. I didn't believe them. However, Summit was telling families of the quarantine and giving them the option of bringing their child back home.

It was alright during breakfast on Day 9. As we were getting ready to go, Dawson told us he was leaving and going home. So right then and there, we all had to say goodbye to Dawson. I didn't cry but I was upset. Max seemed more upset because he had been in the hospital all day. Everyone else, I think, was glad we were leaving.

On the bus, Mama C spoke to all of us and told us that Pete had left travel. This meant we wouldn't meet Dannelle or anything. However, we did have a new director and as she spoke, Mama C told us that *she* was now the director of Summit Travel. Across from me I saw Carl. I saw a tear run down his cheek. I couldn't help but sit in the empty seat behind him and talk to him. He said he was alright. I took a nap and when I awoke, we were at a new lodging.

We were now going to stay at Hyatt. Mama C had arranged this and told us that this place was "Mama C-ita approved". When we went in, we were all amazed. There was a waterfall machine, flat-screened TVs, and it looked so clean. Way to go, Mama C! We knew she would be a great director! We had to wait awhile to get our room keys.

When they called out roommates, I heard my name and CJ's name. Upon hearing this, CJ told Gary he didn't know an Aaron. I got the keys and we got to the room. The room was absolutely amazing and was much more comfortable then the dreaded dorms in Colorado Springs. I was still confused by the rooming of Max and Seth. The reason why they were put together is because they were supposedly sick as they were at the doctor's yesterday. We wanted to get switched up but we forgot about it and stayed in our rooms.

We then went down for lunch and went to the outdoor mall they had near the hotel. We went to Jason's deli for lunch and the Hard Rock Café for dinner. Gary told us during the dinner the truth about Pete: he quit. He felt that the tour should've been stopped and if it went on, he would quit. As for Dawson, I didn't hear but I think in was for personal reasons. It took a while for me to sleep as CJ had the TV on pretty late.

We had Sam's for breakfast on Day 10. We then got ready for the day and went to the elevator. When we got there, Gary introduced us to our new counselor: Nicole. She worked at camp on the waterfront staff and subbed for Debbs on her days off. She came with her husband, Michael, who does soccer at camp. Michael now held the position that Mama C used to have as a floater.

On this day, we went to the Denver Zoo. Grouping was free but I stuck with Gary, Nicole, Max, Seth, Eli, Byron, and Otto. It was nice seeing the animals. After lunch, I started having heart palpitations. Gary stood with me as I called my mom who then called Dr. Steve. For the rest of the trip, I was fine.

Gary and I went by the meet spot. Once everyone was together, we went to the IMAX theater and saw something on the Grand Canyon. I don't know why but I slept. When we exited the theater, it was pouring. We then hung in our rooms and waited for dinner. CJ and I went to get our pizzas from Pizza Hut.

That night, we had the option to either swim in the pool or watch *Watchmen* thru the hotel's system. Max and I were going to watch the movie but then Max changed his mind and asked to go back to his room. I didn't leave just yet but when Michael found out that *Watchmen* was a little under three hours, I asked to leave. So I sat in my room alone with a bad headache.

The counselors came back and I told Gary and Mama C that I had a headache. Gary came by my room and I gave him any of the over-the-counter drugs I had that I couldn't hold. I took two pills of something and went to bed shortly after.

Day 11 saw us treated to Einstein's Bagels by Gary. Although it was the Gary-Nicole group now, Nicole had the day off. So today was a free morning and afternoon. We shopped around and rode around on the city bus.

When we were at Walgreens, I came up with the idea for us to get a birthday card for Mama C since it was July 4. We did so and decided the card would have sound. The one we chose and that Gary liked got me worried that it would offend her. The card said things about being stressed on it.
When you opened the card, it said

"Beer helps"

The card then played "Under Pressure" by Queen and David Bowie. We got back to the hotel and spotted Mama C. Her reaction to the card was priceless and she thanked and hugged us all. Gary had us email our parents. I sent an email to my mom, my school social worker, and Julie (who was still at camp and we emailed on Facebook shortly before the year began).

For lunch, we stopped at Johnny Rockets. Across the street was a Barnes and Noble. We went there and I bought a copy of *Watchmen*, the graphic novel. Soon after, we went on our way to a lacrosse game. It rain at first but we got to see the very boring game. After the game, fireworks were shown. I was with Max and Carl during this. It was intense but nice. Also earlier that day, Mama C noted to put Max and I together.

We were at Einstein's again for breakfast on Day 12. We left the Hyatt that day as well. According to Mama C, Hyatt loved us so much that they gave us three free nights. Still we left and I got to take a nice nap. We went to the Buffalo Bill museum. It was very nice. Next, we took a long ride into the YMCA of the Rockies. Sleeping didn't work because the bus decided to watch *Ghostbusters*.

We had a picnic lunch and then got to our rooms. I roomed with Max, CJ, Joe, and Joseph. I feared the worst. We were in bunk beds. Max and I shared one, Joe and Joseph shared another, and CJ got a queen sized bed. Dinner was at the YMCA itself and it wasn't to my liking.

Shortly before any evening activity, some of the guys were horsing around. Joseph was in the bathroom and the door was locked. We had one key and I decided to hold it since Mike gave it to me. CJ asked for the key and to avoid him bugging me, I gave it to him. He opened the door successfully but Joseph closed the door right after.

Next, CJ took a cup and filled it with foam soap and CJ pretended it was jizz. He wanted to give this to Joseph but had to open the door. I gave CJ the key again and this time, the key broke. CJ stayed behind to pay for another one.

We had a karaoke night. Joseph had asked me if he could use my iPod doc to sing a song. I went down to my room with Nicole and got it. I got to speak with her too. Joseph thanked me and told me he owed me one. My favorite performance that night was Ted's rendition of "Bad to the Bone". To my surprise, my roommates didn't go crazy. We all got along, listened to Steve Martin, and went to sleep.

Day 13 began with us having food in a box for breakfast. I ate everything in there. After breakfast, I went down to the laundry room to dry my damp clothes that I had washed the day before.

Around 10 am, we did the walls and ropes activity. I was with Gary, Max, CJ, Otto, and Andrew from Tim and Beth's group. Mama C had us meet up somewhere and we had a BBQ.

Afterwards, we got on the bus and went to find somewhere to eat for dinner. We went to Chicago Pizza. Our lodging was at Boulder Outlook. I had to talk Max into swimming in the pool there, which was warm.

We had a buffet breakfast buffet on Day 14. I was sitting with Max, Carl, and MC (Carl's co-counselor that trip). As a surprise, we went to a place called Fun & Games (not to be confused with the one near Summit). Nicole, Max, Otto, and I went miniature golfing without keeping score. My average was a four. Otto and I were able to get our golf balls into this ball return box and got special tickets. I got a free game. I spent some time in the arcade. With my tickets I got a back scratcher, a necklace, and some candy.

We had another picnic lunch and had a long bus ride to our next place. *Friends* played but I managed to get my copy of *The*

Dark Knight played. All summer long, I entertained both trips to my impersonation of Heath Ledger's Joker. I had only seen the movie a year ago and it's also one of the very few movies I own from the 21st century. I especially loved to act out the scene when the Joker wants his phone call.

We then went to the Hot Springs pools and had pizza there. The pool was really nice. It was real water without chlorine. There was also a therapy pool, where they had these chairs. When Carl sat in one, I heard him say,

"O-M-Gene Bell"

I laughed and asked him to repeat it because I thought that was one of the funniest things I'd ever heard. In case you don't know, Gene Bell works at Summit and has been doing this since 1999. Gene's job isn't really known except that he booked the hotels. Also when he takes pictures, it's usually when the camp is eating. For the whole summer, I made the joke to take pictures of us eating and see if Gene likes them!

Anyway, we finished up my movie and they put in the second *Fantastic Four* film. We got to the Double Tree hotel much earlier than we thought. Max and I were roommates once again. I got a shower and then we went to bed.

We had another buffet breakfast on Day 15. I noted that I got up early to shave. On this day, we went on a two-hour ride to Utah. Mama C was excited about our next visit because we were going to the Arches. It was really nice but it was very hot. After seeing a short film, we went out to the Arches but not for long because it was so hot.

For lunch, it was another picnic lunch. When we got back to Colorado and to the hotel, we got changed into our bathing suits and swam in the pool. Our dinner was going to be right there but a power outage stopped us for thirty minutes. The BBQ dinner worked out and later on, I went with Max to buy some chocolate cover pretzels. We split them. Gary later took the whole group minus Joe, Joseph, and Otto to a little food store. I got chocolate milk and an issue of *People* magazine with Michael Jackson on the cover.

Day 16 had us leaving Double Tree and moving on. I almost forgot my water bottle and I ran up to get it. For the first half of our ride, we watched *Coming to America* despite its R rating. For lunch, we went to Denny's and left there around 1pm. For the two to three hour ride, *A League of Their Own* played.

Gary let me use his laptop and get some pictures on my memory stick. We then stopped at the Anazani Culture Center. It was alright. It was hard to take seriously because they said in the video if we are to take anything, we should take it with our hearts. It would've been a disaster had we not found a book of birdcalls.

We then got to the Baymount Inn. Max and I roomed once again and would for the entire trip. We had a problem with our keys but with Beth's help, we got in. We went downtown. Nicole and Mike took us to the Main Street Brewery. It wasn't that great. We then saw a Native American dance show.

When we were about to leave, Nicole came running to Mama C and told us they were doing a friendship dance and that we should try to take part. I didn't take part but a few did. That night, Max and I watched *A Hard Day's Night*.

Day 17 was brutal. We got up at 5am and had a small breakfast. We then went to a place called Mild & Wild, a place that took you on white-rapid water rafting. I was worried whether or not I was going to do it. After Nicole and Mama C talked me into it, we were off. I was in a raft with Nicole, Mike, Max, Eli, Jack and Joe from Ted and Lisa's group (originally Ted and Amanda but Amanda left Day 13) and David from Carl and MC's group.

It was okay for the first part. I got pretty pissed when I got wet when I was told I wouldn't. Well, I had to expect it. Joe did bug the hell out of me. He was having fun but being the mood I was in, I felt like taking the sharpest object and going after him with it. My shoes were soaked but no fear: everyone got to go into their bags and get their flip-flops. At a park area, we had another picnic lunch.

Then we started our six hour ride to Flagstaff, Arizona. With *Friends*, *Fun With Dick and Jane*, then *Transformers* playing loudly and girls gossiping behind me, I knew it would be a very long ride. After a few hours, we stopped at the Four Corners. There, I got some flatbread with cinnamon. It was really good. As for the rest of the ride, I had been writing the lyrics to my concept album, *Travelin' Inn* (which I finished a few days later). We got to our second Best Western. Max and I got to our room and the room kind of smelled.

Day 18 was when Max and I got up a little late for breakfast. I was able to watch *The Soup*, a TV show that I love, despite a small interruption. We were just told that Ethan of Ted and Lisa's group had gone home and soon will Joe of the same group. Reasons weren't said. Max and I did watch *Annie Hall* since I got the DVD player to hook up with the TV.

The Gary-Nicole group went to Quiznos for lunch and then we were off to the Grand Canyon. There was a gift shop and I bought these magnetic zingers. Next, we went to the IMAX theater. I didn't have any earplug nor were there any on the bus. I hung out with Tim and we browsed in the gift shop. I got gifts for my mom and sister. For dinner, we went to Sizzler's. I sat at a table with Max and Seth. It was nice. Seth is a really great guy too.

We had breakfast on time on Day 19. That morning, Max and I watched *Born to Boogie*, a T.Rex film. We went to Walnut Park that day. There was a hike and in fear of my heart problems, I stuck with Gary and Otto along with others. I got a nice video of the Travel group yelling "Summit!" on the mountains.

We had another picnic lunch and things got crazy when Mama C had us try something: the counselors would be the campers and the campers would be the counselors. It was nuts. We also walked and hiked at Wupatiki. We also did our laundry as a whole. Dinner was at Sizzler's again and at night, Max and I watched some of *The Godfather Part II*.

Day 20 was our last day in Flagstaff. Our bus ride was five to six hours. For lunch, we had McDonald's. We then went to Lake Meade, where it was extremely hot. I'm not kidding. It was at least 107 to 117 degrees. I went in the water and just had my legs in.

When we got to Las Vegas, it was nice except Max and I had a problem with our room. Like everyone else, we all got switched later that night. We got the chance to go into the city and find a place to eat.

While we walked, I couldn't help but notice the pornographic cards and pictures littered on the street. We were supposed to go to a place called Excalibur's but once we saw the service sucked and that there were exotic dancers on each floor, we went to a food court. It was crazy though. I think it was on this day that I finished up writing my concept album.

Day 21 was the last day of the first trip. Still, we had fun. Breakfast was at a nice little place called Coco's. We then got on the bus and went to an amusement park called Circus, Circus. Circus, Circus is different from other amusement parks as it's indoors. Max and I stuck together as always. We'd bump into a counselor here and there.

For a large part of the day, no one knew where Gary was. When we left at 3pm, we all thanked our driver, Roger, for his services. For dinner, the group plus Mike went to MGM at their Rainforest Cafe. There was confusion with my order but overall it was fine. I finally got to buy a water bottle after losing my first one and loosing the one from Walnut Canyon. This one had the *Survivor* logo on it and it clips on. That way, I wouldn't lose it.

I did get worried at night about how things were all going to go down. I found out that I just might not be with Gary or Nicole. The groups would change. I already knew that of nine people in the group, I was the only one staying for the second trip. The next day would start the bridge trip.

This ends Trip 1. The Bridge Trip is next and shouldn't be too long. Here we go!

We were all woken up early on Day 22. I was told to go on the bus but once I saw Sierra (who was staying for trip 2) stop to say by to everyone on the bus, I knew I was in the wrong place. Beth confirmed that and right there, I hugged Max and said goodbye. I then went to a van where they were taking bags. For the bridge the campers would be Alex, Aden, Ben, Mark, Daisy, and Sierra. The counselors would be Tim, Ted, and MC.

We went to Coco's for breakfast and then the airport. I was in the first flight with Ted, Ben, Alex, and Daisy. The flight from Las

Vegas to Los Angeles was probably less than an hour. We had to wait for Tim and MC with the rest of the campers to come. I had bought a copy of *Rolling Stone* since it was their special issue on Michael Jackson.

Once we were all there, Ted got the rental van and we were off to Best Western Suites. I found out that I would room with Aden. I had told Gary and Nicole my concerns about rooming. MC pulled me aside and she said he was quiet. Although our room was switched because we had a fold out bed, the rooms were amazing. My DVD player could hook up to the TV and there was a couch in the room. I was impressed.

We went to In N Out Burgers for lunch. For the rest of the day, we chilled in our rooms. Around 8pm, we all went to Ted's room and had Subway. It was alright. Ted remembered that I had a DVD player so I went to get it and we watched some of *Back to the Future* because we were all tired. Also, Ted's brother stopped by since he lived in the area.

Day 23 started off with a nice breakfast but early in the morning, I had bad acid reflux. Tim and MC were trying to help me and they did by putting the things I want to bring in my bag. I got to sit in the front of the van and sleep. We went to Santa Monica beach. There, I slept. People were asking me if I was feeling better. Tim and MC brought over lunch. On the beach, I listened to both Love and the Doors.

We did get to walk on the pier and go to the shops. For dinner, it was Barney's Beanery. The place had some rock history behind it, which I liked. I saw in their menu that on the cover of Big Brother's album, *Cheap Thrills*, there's an illustration of the restaurant. We then went shopping. We went to Barnes and Noble. I bought Michael Jackson's *Thriller* and Frank Zappa's *Them Or Us*.

We shopped in a few more places. When Ted had a look at my selections, he told me he bought *Freak Out!* back in the day. From what I noted, I enjoyed *Thriller* on my first listen.

Day 24 was an exciting day. That day, we went to Paramount Studios. We were given a guided tour. At the start of the tour, we were all asked our favorite movies. I said my favorite was *The Godfather*, which I finally saw a day after I turned 17. The guides kept that in mind and we got to stop by the place where a scene was filmed. It was the scene where Michael kills Solonzo and the police chief in the restaurant. That made my day!

We had lunch at McDonald's and then made our way to CBS studios. We were supossed to be in the studio audience for the new ABC Family sitcom, *Ruby and the Rockets*. For some reason, they screwed up and we couldn't get in. It was overbooked and I can see why: the big star in the show was former teen idol David Cassidy. Oh well.

Tim, Ted, and MC then decided we would go to the Hollywood Walk of Fame, although we were to do so on Sunday. We saw some places and got pictures. I got pictures of Michael Jackson's star. It was crowded and there was no security. Also, I went to a place where they sold rock t-shirts. I got one with the New York Dolls on it. For dinner, we went to an Italian restaurant.

Day 25 had us in Venice Beach. However, we all wanted to shop. I decided to invest in a beach towel and I did so. I got a very nice Guns N' Roses towel. After we had lunch, I went back to that place and bought a Frank Zappa t-shirt.

By this time, we were in groups. Groups were by gender so the guys stuck together. I remember a rap group selling their demo to

Alex and Mark. I'm glad they didn't get hurt or anything. These guys looked like they wanted more money out of them.

We relaxed on the beach and then went back to the hotel, where I tried going into a cold pool. I even took an early shower. Soon, we went out to get dinner. Ted had been driving around and around. I remember when we spotted a buffet he said,

"We can go here cause nobody has to bitch about anything. Everybody's happy."

I cracked up along with Daisy. Anyway, I had Pizza Hut. When we returned to the hotel, Aden and I watched *Batman '89*.

Day 26 was supposed to be a surprise. That surprise was going to a LA Dodger's game. For me, that's not a good surprise but whatever. First, we went to the Farmer's Market. We stuck in groups based on roommates so I was with Aden. For lunch we had Johnny Rockets, which was nearby.
Next, we were off to the game. I guess it was alright. The Dodgers won 4-3. We then did laundry, which was just across the street. We were supposed to go to Chili's for dinner but when they were on wait, we went to Denny's instead. That wrapped up our last full day on the Bridge trip. It was now time for trip 2!

Now begins Trip 2. Here we go!

Day 27 saw us packing up and getting ready to leave for San Diego to catch up with the new Travel crew. Once we checked out, we were off. First, we went to Target and then to the Farmer's Market and had lunch right there. We got to browse around. Aden had bought these gummy bears and worms. He gave them to me. I thanked him but that was almost like flushing his money down the toilet.

The ride from Los Angeles to San Diego was a two-hour ride. I tried to sleep. Once we were in the area, we found out we were staying at the University of San Diego. Ben and Mark then started to whine which got Tim a bit mad. I can see why: give the place a chance.

We arrived in the parking lot and all of us got out of the vans. I tapped Carl on his shoulder and he gave me a hug. He and the other counselors had been to camp. From Carl, I found out I was in Gary's group again. His co-counselor was the second person I met up with. Her name was Terra. For a good amount of time, Terra was the unit leader for the lower girl bunks until 2007. She was now back as a counselor on Travel.

Tim, Ted, and MC were leaving. Ted was the only one to say goodbye to me as I remember. We shook hands and all the counselors made sure we got our keys to our rooms. I went upstairs into a lobby of kids all wearing Summit green shirts. Right there, I met Gary once again and he shook my hand.

I found out I was rooming with a guy named Isaac. I put my stuff in the room and made my bed. Isaac was on his iPhone and I remembered him back from camp as he was in the camp newspaper for a short time, I think.

Gary introduced me to the nurse, LaKeisha. Yes, we had a nurse *this* trip. She told me she had earplugs when I needed them and that was good to know. From Gary, I found out the names in the new Gary-Terra group: Aden (different from the bridge trip), Billy, Noah, Nolan, Isaac, Mark, and Seth with two girls, Alison and Sierra (from that first day and the bridge trip).

We had pizza for dinner and then a meeting. After this, we had our own little group meeting just to see if we know each other's names. Isaac and I already had a problem: the lighting in our room sucked. Gary had us move from B202 to B227, which was roomier. Isaac went to sleep but I made sure I got my shower, which everyone was sharing.

I then went to sleep thinking why I signed up for this trip. I tried to think positive and thought to make the best out of it even without a friend like Max. I remember telling Isaac my little story that Gary and I were the only ones and all. Isaac said I'd make new friends...starting with him.

Day 28 started off with us having breakfast in the dining area at the university. Some people who remembered me from Facebook (which I got pretty much anytime) would come up to me and tell me how I didn't look the way I did in my picture on my profile. We then got on a school bus and went to Disneyland. All three groups stayed as they were.

We first went to the California Adventure Park first. Before doing anything, we hit the ATM and Gary explained to the newbies how it all worked. Gary got Sierra and I to go first because we'd done this for 28 days already! While Terra took some of the group on rides, I went with Gary. With us was Noah and several others I didn't note.

We went and took a personality test and somehow, I ended up as Jafar from *Aladdin*. We also got to draw Pluto and then stop by Turtle Talk. Mark was one of the few how got to ask Crush a question. After lunch, Gary squeezed us in to see The Muppet's 3D show. Next, we were off to Disneyland. I got to hang with Terra a bit on a ferry ride. Sierra and the group were enjoying my Joker impression too. As a group, we did go on two rides together: Pirate of the Caribbean and the Buzz Lightyear one. Dinner was alright.

151

Day 29 was the same except we got to chill out for the first half of the day. We had the option of swimming, sleeping, or hanging in the common room. I decided to swim, as did Aden, Terra, and Carl with a few others.

For lunch, we were going to eat at a ballpark because we went to see a Padres game. Now for people who are idiots when it comes to sports, the Padres are a baseball team. It doesn't even take the dumbest person a minute to realize that they are not a good team. Therefore, I started to speak negatively. This got Nolan and a few people pissed off from what I was saying (like that I knew none of the players except that they all had vowels in their names!).

I decided to remove myself from the group because I knew that I had given them a bad impression. When I told Gary what was happening and he was confused when I said I was negative. I think I changed a bit thanks to Travel.

After watching a losing game, we went to the San Diego Zoo. I tried to rub of any bad feelings my group may've had about me. We just enjoyed ourselves and saw some amazing animals. Dinner was there too.

I also made further attempts in meeting up with my mom's brother, Randy. My uncle lives in California and he played in a band for some time. The last time I saw him in person was in 2004 with my grandma. Even before Travel began, I liked the idea of seeing him. It also seemed so fitting and ironic because just a few weeks after I was in California, I was off for my first year at Summit. Long story short, my mom had done the paper work and my uncle told me he'd call Mama C.

On the morning of Day 30, Terra told me that it was official: I was going to meet with my uncle and my cousin (although I didn't know which one yet). Like the other days before, we got packed and left for our next destination: Sea World.

At first, the groups were organized by the group and I ended up in the group I didn't want to be in. That was my fault but it didn't matter. The major highlight was the Shamu show. I had to sit with Mark, who gave me a bit of a hard time. Since we were sitting just one row away from where the wet zone started, he wanted to put his things in my bag. No problem. Then, he requested to *hold* the bag. Oh, jeez!

Lunch was next and for the rest of the day, a large part of the group went on rides. Isaac, Mark, and I were given independence and stuck together. We got to see the walrus and out of my love for Batman and the Joker, we also saw the penguins. By 4pm, everyone was at the meeting spot and left for Denny's. I stayed with Mama C and Mike. Soon after that, we met up with my Uncle Randy. After getting contact info, we were off.

I sat in the back at first but later in the front of the car. Taking the front seat at first was my cousin Cammie, who was three years old. My uncle and I talked while he drove to this place called Cow's, a music store that sold used and new CDs and records. There was some rare stuff but for my first stop, I bought Lou Reed's *New York*.

Next, we went to a Mexican resturant and it was okay. Cammie kept crying and my uncle and the waiters tried just about anything. Next, I took a very quick stop back into Cow's and bought the Faces' *A Nod is as Good as a Wink...to a Blind Horse*.

My uncle then drove me to Target, as I told him I needed some toiletries and wanted a copy of a movie. My uncle helped me find all my toiletries and a copy of *Watchmen* on DVD. Along with an issue of *Rolling Stone*, my uncle offered to pay for it all. I thanked him.

When we were about to leave, my uncle spotted a homeless man. My uncle told me he was trying to get rid of clothes that didn't fit him anymore. He gave this man a jacket. The man thanked my uncle and we went off. My uncle and I both commented that the man looked a lot like Iggy Pop!

My uncle then got us back to the University. When we pulled up, I saw Carl and yelled out his name. Carl and Beth's group all gathered around and it was nice that Carl met yet another member of my family. Terra came by and took pictures. After I said goodbye, I went back up to my room and packed up. Tomorrow, we would be in Hawaii!

It was at 5 am we woke up on Day 31. Our breakfast was similar to the way it had been given when we went rafting in trip one. The whole check in was easy and we got a very nice plane with three sections of sitting.

I sat with Mark and we then started our five-hour flight. I decided to watch *Watchmen* since it would take up a lot of time (I had the director's cut, which is 24 minutes longer and makes it three hours long). While I watched the movie, I had the graphic novel in my hand. It was fun to follow along. The two hours didn't go fast. The plane played *Monsters Vs. Aliens*. That didn't keep me entertained.

When we landed, it was around noon. Long story short, we got to the hotel, which was called the Waikiki Sand Villa. I knew I'd be rooming with Isaac and Nolan but I let Gary know I had bad vibes from Nolan. Gary told me not to worry. He was right. I remember when Nolan had to go back up to get something, he said

"You know, Aaron, you're alright when you're not negative."

Carl happened to pass by and nodded yes in agreement! We went to the ABC stores nearby to pick up a snack or two. We then just chilled in our rooms. There were exactly three separate beds in the room, which was great because cots suck. For some reason, Nolan switched to another room. We got Noah as a replacement.

For dinner, we went to a place called Smorgy's. It had a buffet for all three meals of the day. We then walked to the beach. I spotted a place called The Stupid Factory. When we got back, we used the computers and went in the swimming pool before bedtime.

We didn't expect to have a small breakfast on Day 32. We were told it was continental (which I thought was going to be big like in the hotels on the first trip) but there was hardly anything. We got our bags and headed off to Hawaiian Waters, a water park. It was a lot of fun.

For the first half, I was with Gary and Isaac for the wave pool. It was crazy and got more exciting when I spotted Carl. Our meet point was changed suddenly so since Gary and I were at the original spot, we helped move bags. I think I twisted or pulled a muscle when I carried Seth's bag. He loaded it up with books and shit.

Next, we went to the lazy river. It was alright but it would've been much better if there were rafts. I had really bad sunburn that day. I had sprayed my back and though I rubbed it in (I'm flexible) but I was left with this artsy looking thing. After the water park, we went to a plaza for dinner. Since Isaac and I both wanted to go to

155

Subway, we stuck together. I really thought I had found somewhat of a friend in Isaac. Still, he was on his iPhone most of the time.

Next was a stop at a lagoon. We had the option to swim but since I changed already and didn't like the ocean, I sat there looking at the sunset. Just for fun, I listened to Neil Young's *On the Beach*. I heard it a bunch of times before when I bought it around April but this time, I really liked it. On the ride back, Terra found out that Billy and I had similar music interests and I already knew Aden and I did. I knew Aden since 2005. He was in B14 and next door to me.

Day 33 was a stressful day. On this day, we went on a hike up to a waterfall. We even had plans to have lunch there and then go back down. It was hell. We had to cross little rivers and yes; I had to literally get my feet wet (or in this case, shoes). When we stopped, we weren't even half way and because of the stress, people were at each other's throats and just bitching. We then decided to walk back, go to the beach, and have lunch there.

There was some teen drama in the Gary-Terra group between Aden and Alison. From the start they were always together and on an un-noted day, they made out in the elevator in front of us all (proving Aerosmith right: love *can* happen in an elevator!). They were fine within an hour. The beach was not relaxing at all. We went back to the hotel, hung, and took showers.

Our group went to Smorgy's and celebrated Seth's nineteenth birthday. The night wasn't too good: Gary took a bunch of us to do laundry at the laundry place. I didn't shop or anything. I brought my DVD player and everyone was doing something else so I listened to the CDs I bought a second time. That night, I was listening to *Thriller*. With the music on, I got to talk with Nolan and Billy and just basically chill out. It was nice.

We had a good breakfast on Day 34. We started the day off with going to Turtle Beach. Yes, there were turtles but they were hiding in the ocean. We were told to bring our cameras and not to touch the turtles since they're endangered.

We left for yet another beach. There, we had a picnic lunch. It was hard to get people to head up and get food because they were in the ocean. I couldn't relax after lunch because it was too hot. So I went in the ocean and got my feet wet. I wrote things in the sand such as "O-M-Gene Bell".

When I got bored, I went up and saw there was an ice cream truck. Sierra and Alison had gotten something and said they saw Gary there too. So, I got a milkshake and we ate what was left of the cookies from lunch. Next, we went to get some shaved ice. I chose cherry and grape. It was really good.

For dinner, our group went to a place called Pizza Bob's. There was a little bit of shopping after that and we got back to the hotel. Our group swam in the pool at night.

Day 35 was a surprise when it came to breakfast: Smorgy's. It was nice but I think we were all getting tired of the place! For the morning, we had three things to choose from. One of them was surfing lessons but they charged you $20 to $40. I just hung in and listened to albums I needed to give a second listen. We went downtown and got lunch. I went to Subway.

After lunch, we went on the bus and we were given a tour by our bus driver named Johnny (who was the driver on Day 33 too). Johnny then led us into the Polynesian Center. It was fun. In our groups, we went to different places such as Samoa and Fiji. In short, it was kind of like Epcot without Disney. At 5 pm, we had our dinner at a lauo and got real leis. For the night, we saw a show called *Ha*. It was pretty amazing, especially the fire dancers.

We got up early on Day 36 for the Pearl Harbor memorial. When we got in, there was a little museum. I got to hang with Carl before we got into the theater to see a short film. I feel asleep.

Finally, we got on the ferry and went to the actual memorial. It was nice and a little hard for some, as Aden had found his grandfather's brother on the list of the people who died. Next, we went to the Swap Meet. It was basically a flea market. I stuck with Noah. We had lunch there too. I bought myself a Hawaiian shirt for $10. We got back to the hotel and relaxed for a bitFor dinner, we went to Jimmy Buffet's diner. It was alright. For desert, we went to Hagen-Daaz.

Day 37 had us leaving Honolulu and flying to Hilo. It was a quick flight. We even got to use the Internet at the airport only we had to pay money (five minutes a dollar). We got on a coach bus and arrived early at our lodging, Uncle Billy's (or Hilo Bay). I knew it since yesterday that I was going to room with Billy.

We had our lunch, which was awful. We all got folders that said we were a part of a program called EDventure. A hip-hop dancing group called Shell Shock Crew performed. They then taught some moves to some campers. In return Carl led a group, including me, into dancing to "Proud Mary". It felt like old Summit Camp. I almost cried.

We then got to our rooms and took early showers. Billy had the same taste in music as me so there should've been no problems. There were a few. I couldn't get control of the TV. He couldn't even settle on one channel. He kept surfing.

Anyway, we went to a place called Ken's for dinner. I was unaware that we would be eating there for our whole entire stay. It rained also. When we got back to the hotel, I made further attempts in socializing with Billy. I had him look at my iPod and I let him listen to whatever but he was surprised that I had so much AC/DC. He said he had a hard time looking online (buy the CD!).

Day 38 was our first full day with the EDventure program. We went to a place called the Imiloa, an astronomy place. For the first half, we stuck as one big group and it was weird at first. We saw some short thing and a show about how the Big Bang Theory was like an apple pie.

The highlights of the day were a 4D show and a planetarium show, which I slept through. To my surprise, I actually got something in the gift shop. It was this collection of magnetic acrobats. I remember getting something like that from my dad. It got me so I bought the thing.

Coconut Beach was next. We had another bad lunch. We then got to do different activities. I went fishing and it was fun although I didn't catch anything. I kept joking around with saying something from a Bert and Ernie skit on *Sesame Street*. In the skit, Bert and Ernie are fishing. Bert can't catch anything so Ernie tries to help by teaching him by learning a call. The call went like,

"Heeeeere fishy, fishy, fishy!"

When Ernie did this, a bunch of fish hopped into the boat. So, I said this while fishing and a couple of people picked up on it. Beth found it funny.

At 3 pm, we got back to our rooms. Billy was still flipping channels so I told Gary and Terra what was going on and that I wasn't trying to tattle or whatever. Terra spoke to Billy and me both. She said to agree on shows and make this a good friendship. It helped a little as I did get to see *Seinfeld* without any flipping. Billy was on his cell phone for a long time, which made it a bit difficult to socialize with him then.

For dinner, it was back to Ken's. I sat at a table with Eli, Dylan (both of Carl and Beth's group), and Peter (from Nicole and Lisa's group). It was awkward. I mean, I'm shy but the things they talked about...I couldn't relate. Sitting the table next to us was this elderly couple. Dylan kept leaning over me to speak with them. He did ask if I minded this. I lied and said no. Luckily, I got out of my seat as Gary wanted to ask me who Jimmy Carl Black was.

On Day 39, we had a nice breakfast with cereal added. In the morning, we went to the Farmer's Market in Hilo. I stuck with Aden, Nolan, and Noah but mostly Noah as Aden and Nolan were off everywhere. I did get a wooden necklace of a lizard. The highlight of being there was seeing this man preaching in the streets. Everyone just stared at him.

We went to Akaka Falls, which was very nice despite the rain. For lunch, we were at the place where the 1946 tsunami occurred. There were fantastic views of the ocean there. The water would just crash onto the rocks. It was beautiful. Soon after, we went back to the hotel and took quick showers.

We got to Ken's early because we were doing something later that night. That something was a Bon Dance. From what I know, it's basically line dancing except you dance around in a circle. It's popular in Japan. Carl tried it and he loved it. I joined in with others. It was really fun and got a bit silly at times.

It rained also but we didn't really care. At 9 pm, we saw these drummers who were amazing. I got a few comments from people thinking I looked like Ike from Carl and Beth's group. It was the first time anybody told me I looked like another camper since my first year in 2004, when most people thought Trent and I looked alike. I found it kind of creepy.

Day 40 had us eating breakfast in a bigger room. On this day, we went to the Hawaii Volcanoes. Our tour guide, Claudia, told us all about them. Lunch was at a picnic area and I spoke with Carl a bit. He told me that last night; it looked like I was really enjoying my group. He was right and they beat out ST12 from session 2 of last year. Still, I hadn't found a friend exactly.

Anyway, we went to the Jaggar Muesum, the Lava Tubes, and an Orchird shop. As for the night, it was the Same drill as the days before. At Ken's, we had a big table of people all from the Gary-Terra group.

Towards the end of our stay, Gary was confused to see that most of our table all had desserts. They also went over their bill, which both Gary and Terra were not happy about. Gary then took Sierra, Billy, Noah, Mark, Eli, and I out to get ice cream (although Mark left and didn't want any). Gary felt that we shouldn't suffer because of them so he paid for the ice cream. When we got back to the hotel, Billy and I did our laundry.

Day 41 had us at the Macadamian Nut Factory. It was really nice and interesting how they all got processed. We were given free samples off the bus and I kind of liked them. I thought about getting some but figured to save my money for San Francisco. Also, I was constipated. Gary was aware of this (Terra had the day off but I told her the next day). I hadn't gone in days but for the day, I was fine. People who bought nuts had to pack them up because one of the

161

campers (I know who it is. I'm not saying here) was deathly allergic to them.

Next, it was off to the Hilo Zoo. Aden had been advised to spend time with other people besides Sierra, Alison, and Nolan. Aden asked if he could come with me and I agreed. So Aden and I saw a bunch of animals. Aden liked this one parrot and worked with her so well. I got a video of him speaking to the bird in Spanish and another later in the day of him doing a rap with the bird. The bird actually danced!

Lunch was at the zoo and we then went to a bowling alley. It was stressful at the beginning. Scores had to be kept on confusing overhead-projecting scoreboards. In the end, it was worth it. We went to the mall next and went to the movies.

I saw *Harry Potter and the Half-Blood Prince*. I was already hearing bad things about it, which kind of ruined it for me but it was good. I did a little shopping in the mall. I just bought a blue Led Zeppelin t-shirt at Spencer's.

Gary had the day off on Day 42, so Terra was in charged. In the morning, we went to the Kuloa Center. It's a place where elderly people go to and sometimes show younger people how to create things. The groups were split into four: girls and three boy groups based on counselors. So the eight guys in the Gary-Terra group first made wristbands and then a straw-like bracelet. We then learned two hula dances and ended it with Ukulele lessons. In return, we presented the elders with the Summit "Proud Mary" dance.

For lunch, we had Pizza Hut there and we were off to go canoeing. It was raining. When we were moving our bags, I had my umbrella opened. It accidentally hit a camper (just a tiny bit) named Mary Grace (who was disrespected and hated by her peers throughout the trip). She had a freak-out and it kind of scared me although she did not intimidate me at all.

Terra said because I arrived later when she called the group, I'd be going in the last group to canoe. When I told her I wanted to get it done with, she thought I had a temper in my voice. I told her I was stressed out and she talked to me and gave me a hug.

I ended up deciding not to go in a canoe. As with the nights before, the drill was the same. At Ken's I sat with Sierra, Alison, Aden, Nolan, Isaac, Mark, and Ike. I remember Ike telling me I could be the next Joker. That was nice to hear because I knew I'd be rooming with him in San Francisco.

Day 43 was a traveling day as we were leaving Hawaii and going to San Francisco, California. We checked in and chilled. Before the flight, Beth came up to me with Ike and asked if we knew each other. We sure did. Ike told me he had *The Dark Knight* and a DVD player. I told him I had the same. Gary and Beth laughed and remarked that we should be good roommates.

Gary had explained to me the reason why I was with Ike was because both of us couldn't agree with people from our own group when it came to rooming. I mean I liked my group very much but Gary was right. I thought I could room with Aden but they surprisingly put with Ike, which I was absolutely fine with. In fact, I think he belonged in our group.

Anyway, the first flight was short. I was with Sierra on the first flight. We had a little time in between before the second flight to San Francisco. I didn't like lunch last time on the plane to Hawaii so I got Pizza Hut at the airport. For the five-hour flight, I would be sitting next to Aden. We really got to talk and socialize. To fill up three hours, we watched *The Godfather*. I tried to relax and listen to my iPod.

An in-flight movie played, which was *Ghosts of Girlfriends Past*. I didn't watch it. The flight was a bit delayed for landing. When we landed, I was so happy. We found our bus and the ride from the airport to Travelodge (our lodging). I remember being in the back of the bus and Ike, Aden, Sierra, Alison, and Nolan were all there. Ike was jokingly making jacking off gestures. I commented,

"So that's why it took so long for us to land"

Ike laughed and gave me a high five. Good joke. We got to the hotel and then our rooms. Gary brought pizza to our room. Ike and I did talk a bit. He was unpacking some of his stuff. We talked a little I think but we watched *Family Guy*. Around 12 or 1, we went to sleep.

Day 44 had me wake up in pain. Long story short, let's say that I was a happy camper once the pain was gone. I took a shower and then Ike and I went to breakfast.

For this day, we would be going to downtown San Francisco. We stayed in our groups. The Gary-Terra group walked a little and then went on the trolley. After one too many stops, we got off at Pier 39. We split into little groups and agreed to meet at the Hard Rock Cafe. Aden, Billy, Nolan, and I stuck together.

We went to a few shops, one of them being a place called Antiques. It had records and posters signed by musicians and actors. They had two different shops. In their smaller one, I bought a deck of Beatles playing cards. We then ate lunch at Hard Rock.

Next, we went to *Ripley's Believe It or Not* Museum. It was fun. After that, we went to a penny arcade that had really old games probably from the 1930's and later. After seeing the sea lions a second time, Gary and I went to Antiques.

For some weird reason, I still had $400 left on my debit card. I bought a tie-dye Beatles t-shirt with a silhouette of them crossing *Abbey Road* and a fabric poster of Black Sabbath.

For some reason, the bus we were scheduled to go on back to City Hall was full. A limo pulled up and its driver told the crowd he went to different places. It was five dollars a person. We had twelve people so $60 sounded good.

I made some crazy videos of us in the limo. There were two other people in it and got out very soon for their destination. We were nuts and since we were early, we terrorized a playground and I got another video or two.

We got back on the bus and passed by Haight-Ashbury. For dinner, we went to the IHOP next door. It was just our group who went. I got back in the room and saw Ike turned off the lights except the bathroom light. He said hello and I went in the corner to write and record. He was on his cell phone. He then asked me,

"Aaron, do you have a girlfriend?"

I told him no. He said he was on the phone with his girlfriend, who was on the first trip. It was very hard to socialize at this point. I'm not really good friends with people my age who have significant others.

He eventually hung up and repeated the same question to me. I gave him the same answer and then asked if I want one. I basically told him what I told too many: I needed more friends of my gender and then see what happens. I had told him the night before about my dad passing away.

Long story short, Ike and I talked till about midnight. I had done what I thought I could never do in my six summers with Summit: socialize well with someone outside my bunk or group.

Day 45 was a really cool day. I remember at breakfast, I told Carl about how Ike and I were getting along fine. He told me he knew we would get along. We went to the Exploratorium on this day. It was really nice. It reminded me of the Discovery Museum back where I lived.

I mainly stuck with Ike, Sierra, and Alison. Some of my favorite things I got to do that day include making huge bubbles and a microphone that picked up on your voice and see how a crowd would react. I got videos of both.

We were the second group to go into this dome. You had to be careful because it was pitch black in there. You would have to go with three other people and use your hands as eyes. It was fun and I did it four times.

The third or fourth time I did it was going ahead solo with Carl helping Mama C complete it. They cheated with using a flashlight on the walkies but Mama C really wanted to do this. Hearing them talk and work their way out would've been a dream for a guy who used "that's what she said" every two minutes. Carl was funny, as he exchanged old sayings since I was with him. I can remember after climbing the ropes in there, Carl said, "Dirty". I cracked up that he took one of my catchphrases.

We had lunch there too and stayed there until 4pm. Some counselors had the night off while the rest of us went bowling. I won in my group with a score of 120...with the bumpers! I wanted them gone. We had pizza there and that was our dinner.

We got back early too at like 7pm. Terra had a bunch of us do laundry. Terra had Sierra and I getting change for $20 at two places. We went to the gas station and the IHOP. Both were no help except the guy at the gas station offered three bucks in quarters. Jeez, I can see them getting really far in life...bastards!

However, Terra allowed Sierra and I got our laundry done second because we worked so hard. I told Ike what happened and he said that it was bullshit that no one would give us quarters! I had to stay at the laundry for a while but since it was close by, I got to run back and forth.

That night was a bit crazy. When the lights were out, Ike was still on the phone with his girlfriend. I then heard and saw these movements. He spoke on the phone,

"Yeah...I'm not making any noises like other guys...Ready...Give it to me...keep going."

I whispered to Ike and he got pissed. I shut up and he continued. It was pretty obvious what was going on: Ike was having phone sex. I left it as that. Obviously, we weren't going to chat!

I woke up early on Day 46. Ike woke up also and apologized about last night. I told him it was fine and joked we all get crazy at one point in our lives. I'm still trying to figure out what I meant!

On this day, we went to Alcatraz. It was really cool. We went on the boat to the prison, went up, and went inside. The tour was basically an audio tour, which I loved. My mom and dad liked doing audio tours. The place was so cool and had so much history. I heard many interesting stories.

The best part of going there was going to the gift shop and meeting a man named Jerry Wheeler. Wheeler was a guard at the prison for two years and just happened to be a Pearl Harbor veteran. He told us he was turning 88 years old soon. He was there because the prison was celebrating their 75th anniversary. We got a few pictures with him and thanked him. What a guy and not all of Travel met him.

We had lunch back at Pier 39 because it was very close. We lost Aden, Alison, Billy, Noah, Nolan, and Sierra for ten minutes. The bus wasn't where was supposed to be. They didn't know. Next, we went to Redwoods. They had some huge trees. The ride back to the hotel was hell but there were so many antics at the back of the bus (where I was). Aden kept us entertained, for sure. Mama C then split us into small groups to go to IHOP. Ike, Nolan, Isaac, Alison, and I went in one group. The service was really bad that night as there were only two people working there.

Day 47 was our last full day. We had breakfast and went on the bus. For the entire day, we went to Westfield Mall. We were early so we looked around and then got into the mall at 11 am. The first few minutes there were scary and weird. While we were waiting, Aden and Billy were arguing and then they got physical. So physical that Billy ripped one of Aden's sleeves off his shirt. It got really bad. This wasn't a first. When we went bowling in Hawaii, they got in each other's faces. This was worse.

Upon seeing this, I yelled "Hey! Stop!" loud enough for Gary and Terra to hear. Mark and I split them up until the counselors came. Gary and Terra were not happy, that was for sure. Gary took the six of us (Isaac and Nolan were off somewhere) and we went to the Borders in there.

We took the elevator. Mark was doing his best at navigating us. When we were at one floor, a hobo walked in and saw that Mark had pressed a button twice. The guy went nuts and insulted him by slurring,

"You don't press it twice. You a fucking idiot. You a fucking idiot, man"

Luckily, the hobo got off. Gary had told Mark to not say anything. When he walked out of the elevator, I said,

"No, sir I think you are mistaken. You are the fucking idiot."

We then talked about it on the way out. Gary thought the man was just very messed up and ill. I was thinking the same thing. When we got to Borders, Mark started whining about nothing. We just went inside. Luckily, there was a music store. I still had I a hell lot of money on my debit card so I just thought "Go crazy...but not too crazy" because whatever remained was my mom's gift. Even if she didn't ask me for it, I would've given her all her money back. She deserves it.

Anyway, I bought three things. I bought Michael Jackson's *Number Ones* (yes, a compilation. I had a strange liking to hear "Black Or White." Even after the trip, I bought both *Off the Wall* and *Bad*), Yes' *The Yes Album*, and surprisingly a copy of the movie *Network*. I had seen it a day before Travel started. I really liked it and had been telling Gary I wanted a copy of it. I didn't see it in drama but ironically enough, I found it in comedy. Next, Noah and I went to the food court and had pizza. Sitting behind us was Aden and Billy, who had made up. Jeez, that was fast!

Noah and I then went to Hot Topic next. I bought a Velvet Underground shirt and a copy of Danzig's debut album (yes, they have music just not a good selection). Noah and I went back to Borders and met up with Gary. Gary knew I wanted a memory stick so that I could get more pictures from him.

He took a large group of us to go outside the mall. We went to Game Stop first since they didn't have one in the mall. Next, we went to Walgreens. There, I got a 2 GB memory stick. It turned out to be really cheap but it actually worked!

Lastly, we went to a music store called Rasputin's. I expected it to be big and all but it wasn't that big. Their music selection was cheap and they had only one floor for music but we didn't have time. So I bought Iggy Pop's *Lust for Life* and a CD case for all the CDs I bought to take some weight off my back.

We left the mall and went back to the hotel. Originally, we going to go to IHOP but Mama C changed her mind. We all packed up for tomorrow and then got to use our electronics. For dinner, we had what they called a "pasta picnic". It was okay. I listened to all my purchases from that day and some of my previous ones.

Again, Ike was on his phone but I showed him my new things. In fact, I just played the famous "I'm as mad as hell..." scene from *Network* just to see how a person nearly my age (Ike was going into eleventh grade) reacted. He laughed and suggested I do whatever Howard Beale had told his viewers to do. I had said it before but as the Joker (if you get that joke, pat yourself on the back). That night, I got pictures from Gary. I told him I was worried. He told me everyone gets it. I just had to sleep.

On the morning on Day 48, Ike and I got up and lugged our suitcases out before we had breakfast (or after. I'm not sure). Ike was telling me that I had left a full can of Sprite out that night. I laughed and told him it was too early. When we were on the bus, Ike reminded me again.

"The maid can have it as her tip" I said.

Nolan laughed. It was a good joke for such a sad day. We got to the airport. My bag weighed in at 48.5 pounds. I was carrying my Summit bag to hold my CD cases!

I got a little bit of a meal but at 10 in the morning, I thought no one would give me a slice of pizza. I was supposed to sit with Billy on the flight but things got switched and ironically, I sat next to Sierra with Mark (of Carl and Beth's group) on my left. It was going to end the way it sort of began.

On the five-hour flight to Newark, I watched *Network* and loved it. On the plane were televisons on the back of every seat via DirectTV. Luckily, we could swipe our debit card and watch television. I made sure I got to see *Seinfeld* and *Family Guy*.

When we landed, some of the parents were there at the gate. At baggage claim, I saw my mom and hugged her. Once I had my bag my mom gave her tips to Gary, Nicole, and Terra. I said goodbye to all of them and I made sure I didn't forget Carl. Carl told me something like this,

"Aaron, you took Summit steps last year. This year, you took Summit leaps. I'm proud of you."

I tried my best to hold back my tears. When my mom and I were in the elevator, I cried. When I got home and saw all the furniture, I cried. It wasn't like camp when I came back as I had stayed in one spot for eight weeks. This time, I had been all over the country. I was also crying because I didn't know if this was still truly my last year with Summit. Could I go just one more year? I felt awkward but later, I had to admit: it was good to be home.

I've gotten to speak with Max on the phone after Travel. In October, I turned eighteen years old. As for a seventh year, it won't be happening. I was accepted to King's College around November and I will be doing their five week summer program for freshmen. In June, I will graduate from high school. While I hate and have to think about college, I try to put it aside.

I'd like to see my sixth year as coming of age. I'll be okay with not going to Summit again. For five years and six summers, Summit Camp and Travel have had a special place in heart.

I've been with 53 bunkmates and two girls in those six summers. So, I've known a total of 55 people and no matter what; all of them have made a lasting impression. I've also had 18 wonderful counselors. All of them helped me during the hardest times.

I think that no matter which camp a kid goes to, it will build their character. Summit did that for me. Although Summit Camp has changed a lot after 2008, I wouldn't mind paying a visit. I'm grateful for Summit and it will forever be a major highlight of my life.

THE END!

Introduction to the revisits

As I got older, it became more and more difficult to understand my first two years at camp. Remember, I was very young when I wrote them. I felt as if my work was already done with writing those essays and keeping them the way they are. I then got the idea to revisit the first two years of camp and write them in the present day as a young man rather than a young teenager.

The reason why I put these in the end and not the beginning is because of my writing growth. If you read all six seasons/essays, you can see a clear writing growth. Personally, I find that cool to see how much better one person gets over the years. Had I replaced the original essays with the new ones, the feel would've been different. I hope you enjoy reading these revisits. I had a lot of fun writing them!

The Camp: Season 1 Revisited
By Aaron Conn

It was 2004. I was 12 years old and wasn't happy with the idea of going to a sleep-away camp. I was thinking it was going to be horrible. I decided that I'd keep a journal. What would I write about? I would write about the torture and harassment that I would go through. Also, I was anxious so I thought I could cry myself home.

As it turned out, I enjoyed my time at camp and by 2009, I'll be there ending my tenure with my sixth year. The idea of *The Camp* is a great one. The way I've written these essays every year since 2005 are so much different not only in length but by use of vocabulary. I'll try to revisit the summer of 2004.

It was July 27, 2004. I remember I was twelve years old and was anxious about going away for a number of weeks to a sleep away camp. Summit Camp was a special camp for kids who had learning disabilities and the things that come with it. I was with my mom and my paternal grandma. We had lunch at this place, which was a hotel. Other campers were waiting to go there. It was cloudy and rainy that day.

I do remember after saying goodbye to my mom and grandma, I sat in this van and started to cry. I tried to stay strong and told a counselor sitting upfront that I was nervous. He said he'd keep an eye on me and I left it at that. So, we then started our long ride to camp. I stayed calm and I think I listened to the first two Kiss albums on my CD player.

When we got to the camp, it was still raining. I remember that my female counselor, Kenda, was waiting for me. I had met her before as long time employee Regina had given my mom and I a tour just weeks ago. She said hello and he walked to the cabin.

On the way there, she asked about my *Survivor* buffs. I told her I was a fan and said I had been a fan since Season 4. I remember she asked who won that season and I told her it was Vecepia. We got to the cabin, where I found my bed. I set my things there. I had the bottom of a bunk bed with a bunk mate named Kyle.

Oddly enough, I remembered Kyle from a day camp I went to. I think I met Kyle around 2000 or 2001. I was thinking while on the tour "This is where he's been all this time?" Kenda and I then walked to computers, where my bunk was. I met Nate, one of my male counselors. He was there on the tour so seeing him again was very nice. The bunk just gestured at me, being polite. I don't remember who was there when but my bunk mates were to be Andrew, Alec, Brandon, Byron, Jaron, and Kyle. We would be the bunk, B12.

Once the bunk was going back to the cabin, I started to get this lump in my throat. I have a major case of anxiety and anytime that happens, I can hardly speak. I tried to tell Nate I was nervous and he said I'd be alright.

So we were in the cabin and there was a counselor there named Jeff, who was my third and final counselor. He said hello. I was just sitting on my bed, looking at everyone. I just decided to get out my CDs and when I got them out, Andrew was very enthusiastic about my music. Jeff and Nate were also wowed. I felt so great then. I was asked which case was which. There was one case alone for Kiss and Andrew just kept saying "Oh, man!" So at that point, I felt great. I didn't shower though. I was too nervous.

I can remember there was one situation involving Byron and he said something weird. I forget what it was but Andrew looked to me and shook his head. I knew what it meant: the bunk didn't approve of Byron. Sooner or later, we had dinner. When I was there, the surroundings were far from the ones at home. Sitting next me was Tom, a specialist who was with woodshop that year. Specialists usually take an extra bed and stay with that bunk. So when I was feeling odd, Tom asked me,

"Are you homesick?"

I nodded my head. He said that I would be fine. Knowing that there was someone who cared just made me feel better. After dinner, we had Horseshoe time. Horseshoe time is the time of the day that campers are free to walk around the camp and mingle. It was called Horseshoe time because a group of cabins lay on the ground that is in the shape of a horseshoe. It's also where the HC Hut was.

Since I was new, Kenda just showed Alec and I what this was. On that evening, we had a movie night. That night, we watched *Billy Madison.* It was PG-13, so I waited outside and my unit leader, Danelle, said she called my mom and my mom said it was okay for me to see the movie. It was amusing. However by the end of the night, Byron was no longer with us. He moved to B10 and from that bunk, we got Trent. He made himself at home to his new bunk. He stood out with his long hair. Andrew did too but he has a Mohawk! In those days, I thought that you could tell a person's taste in music by the length of their hair. It is true sometimes but for the most part, it isn't. Trent would happen to have my tastes in music. We then went to bed. I had a hard time sleeping that night.

I awoke on Day 2 in a cabin and a blanket was hanging over my view. I also found a pair of glasses and gave them to Kyle, who thanked me. That day was another rainy day for the most part, I think. We had chores in the morning and that day I was shown how to clean the shower.

We were supposed to have AI (Athletic Instruction) first but instead, the staff set up board games to play. I was playing Battleship with some kid but every time I looked up, I swear I saw a reflection of myself. It wasn't. It was Trent. For the entire year, people would mistake us as twins or brothers. We had ceramics, discovery, and swimming tests that day.

This was also my first shower. I know how silly that sounds but I was scared. I was first in and I was just scared that someone would find me naked. My plan for the rest of the summer was this: I'd go behind a bathroom stall, have a towel around me and a bathrobe too. I'd go in, hang the towel and bathroom on the upper ledge of the shower. This was so they knew someone was in there. It turned out that Trent and I were the only ones that didn't flash anyone or were caught in the nude!

That night, we got to waiter. This was my first time waitering at camp and it would be the only time that year since STs do waitering. That night, the activity was a sort of getting-to-know you thing. We were told that we'd be living with each other for some time and that we should make it Utopia. We were to have rules and a bunk name, which we called Kajjat Bank. We got it from using the first letter of everyone's first name.

Day 3 was our first trip day. We went to the movies and saw *Spiderman 2*, which I enjoyed. We then had Puppets & Masks and tests for baseball. We also had talent night and before we had it, I took something too sensitively. Andrew was talking to Trent or telling someone that he didn't like the band, The Darkness, who were new at the time. I had heard a song by them and I liked them.

177

"Are you fucking kidding me?" asked Andrew in a negative tone.

I took it way too personally. I spoke with Nate and he said it would be alright. We had a Talent night. All I noted was that the bunk dance and I thought Jeff was funny. In fact, tomorrow he'd be in charge. I wanted him to know about my anxiety and he said he was cool with it and to come to him anytime. He then told me to press thumbs with him.

"I like you" he said.

I felt great and went to sleep. Day 4 was Jeff's day in charge. Nate had the day off and Kenda was sick with pneumonia. Jeanette from B13 subbed her spot for the time being. That day saw me doing great. The campers and counselors all liked me. I had swept the floor in Arts and Crafts. I felt great. We also saw the International Night show. It was basically counselors from the same country dancing on stage in support of their country.

Day 5 saw Kenda with a day off and Nate and Jeff in charge. Keyoshi of B13 was our counselor that day also. He was too funny. I remember going to the bathroom and he was in the other stall making noises. After flushing the toilet, he remarked

"That was a very good pee"

We also had go-carts, jewelry, and used Windows Movie Maker in computers. Day 6 saw the return of Kenda. I, however, had a toothache. We had Drama that day and it was fun. Brandon, Andrew, Trent, and I all worked out a sketch about a rock star going nuts. The evening activity was a gold-stealers night. A bunch of counselors were hiding. The bunk who got the most gold (or thieves, as they ran out of gold) won. We were the winning bunk and we had milkshakes.

Day 7 was wild. We went on a trip that was meant to only be four camp periods of hiking. We were there the entire day! It was an experience though. For instance, our old bunk mate Byron had a fit. This was because we all got to choose different muffins to eat. He wanted a chocolate one but they ran out of them. Just a reminder: This is a group of twelve year old boys! We were blessed that we had Trent instead. For dinner, we had Pizza Hut. Jeff couldn't go because of his back.

Day 8 saw us canoeing. I was in a canoe with Jeff and Brandon. That day was also our bunk photo and for movie night, we finished *Billy Madison* and started *School Of Rock*. Day 9 went quick. I don't think it was because both Kyle and Alec pulled down their pants. Actually, Alec did in front of a bunch of people. With Kyle, he was listening to the Spongebob "F.U.N." song on a disc I made. He then told me to look down and I was scarred for sure.

We had lunch at the tennis court for our picnic lunch, which lower camp had every Wednesday. Trent had gotten a slingshot. Andrew, Trent and I were trying to figure it out. I got hurt but I survived, didn't I? That night, we also watched the rest of *School Of Rock*.

Day 10 was our trip to the mall. I was disappointed in my group as I was with Nate and Jaron. Now I was cool with Nate but I couldn't understand Jaron. He was a bit strange. I'll never forget that day because he had the idea of getting a cell phone if Nate and I combined our money with him. What do we get out of it?

I obviously wanted music. I only had $12. I wanted to purchase a Kiss album (*Hot In The Shade*, to be exact. It was a mediocre album) and it was $14. Nate, seeing my problem, said he'd lend some cash. However at checkout, he gave a $20 to the cashier and I gave him $5. So basically, Nate bought the album. I thanked him gratefully but we had to keep it a secret as counselors weren't allowed to do that.

We had a karaoke night that same day. It was too crazy. I have pictures of it and they bring me back to that crazy night. Day 11 has a very short entry in my journal from then. Nate had the day off and Kenda went to see a sick friend. Jeanette stopped by again. The evening activity was a play based on the music of the Beatles. It was called "Come Together". It was alright.

Day 12 has an even shorter entry! All I said nothing much happened and that I went to computers for clubs. Day 13 was pretty cool. We went mountain biking despite the mud. At the end of the little trip, the other kids had found an orange lizard and a calipiter. Jaron, not knowing, thought the calipiter was dead. So he threw it in the air and stepped on it. I also got to go on the banana boat, which was a cold ride.

We had a hockey night and we lost to B11, I think it was. I kept missing but Jaron messed up being goalie. The bunk got angry at him but I mean, calm down! It's just a game. Also, I was put down by the news of Rick James passing away. Day 14 was Track and Field Day. We were the red team and white won. Still, it was alright. I couldn't run or do too much because I twisted my ankle.

Day 15 had a short entry. I only noted that we saw *50 First Dates* for movie night and that Trent and I went on a paddle boat again. Yes, again. I don't remember the first time! I think the reason I noted these things was because I didn't really have friends outside camp.

Day 16 has a decent entry. I didn't note the things we did. I remember we did practice a dance for our unit play, *School Of Rock*. Trent and I would have these index cards while the bunk danced to the rocking music. As a reward, we camped out in the canteen. I was in a tent with Andrew and Trent. I felt so great, so high on life. Then we had to decide what movie to watch: *Nutty Professor II* or *Hellboy*. I wanted to sleep with laughs so I picked that. After a 4-3 vote, *Nutty Professor II* won. I tried getting back in the tent but Trent was pissed.

"I thought you were one of us" he sneered.

"Trent, just let him in" said Andrew.

Trent left the tent so it was just Andrew and I. So, I wasn't feeling good. I talked to all my counselors. Nate ended it with the fact that Trent would forget about it in the morning. I agreed with that and went to sleep but not in the tent. They had mats outside of the tents.

Day 17 was our trip day. However, it was raining. Before we left, I'll never forget what happened. Jeff was angry that he found an excrement mark on one of the toilet stall doors. He then went into this speech and I couldn't stop laughing. The group for the Wayne County Fair was Jeff, Andrew, and I. Adam from B13 and his group walked along with us. It was still fun.

Day 18 saw B12 as the bunk with the most stars for the week in lower camp. Day 19 and 20 I wrote together because I was sick. We saw an awful *Lord Of The Rings* play from the STs. Day 20 was Alec's birthday. I can't remember which day it was but at this point or earlier, Kyle lost his blue, soft snot-rag. I then suggested that we have a funeral for it and we did.

I still laugh that we had the lights off and Kyle came out of the bathroom with a flashlight and put it down and prayed while Pink Floyd's "Great Gig In The Sky" played! Andrew wrote a song for it that was negative. Jeff also had another song which had me running to the bathroom. The funniest thing is that days later while cleaning up, Kenda found it. Oh well! Day 21 has another short entry and I only noted Kyle peed at boating. I remember the instructor, Ollie, cleaning it telling a kid,

"Try to stay away from the pee"

Day 22 was our only normal Monday as we always had some trip. I also got to call my mom. We had our only splash night. The pool was warm and it was just beautiful.

Day 23 saw Jaron leaving the bunk and moving to B13 since they were missing one person. We were all happy he was gone and out of character, I do remember making a remark that morning that Nate and Jeff weren't happy with. I almost cried outside but everyone one forgot it. The other things I noted were that we finished *50 First Dates*.

Day 24 was our last trip day. We were supposed to go to a water park. It rained and we went to an arcade. I'm not really good with games and you would never see me with tons of tickets. I arrived at this game where you'd have all these hoops with point values. You had to slam your hand hard on the rubbery button to use the catapult-like thing. Anyway, I slam my hand and all the sudden, ticket start coming out…too many of them. I thought the thing was broken and wanted to tell Keyoshi but he was focused on something else.

Ben J. of B13 explained to me that I won the 500 point prize. Brandon, of my bunk, came over and helped me fold them up and find out the total. It was a large number and Brandon gave this big hug because of that! I used it on candy mostly but Kenda helped me spent it all because I had the bus waiting for a short time!

Day 25 was a short entry. All I noted was that we saw the staff play, *Hairspray*. It was great, as written in my journal. Day 26 saw us wrapping up. We did get to watch *Starsky And Hutch*, which was funny. We also saw the slideshow for the second half and I was in it nine times. They make it so depressing at the last day celebrations. The part that got me teary eyed was when they lit the year on fire (the year was made out of old towels and stood on poles that made it a sign). It was very moving.

Day 27 was the last day, of course. Jeff asked B10 for Cooper to have an eye out on me in case I got anxious. Seeing my mom and sister again and just hearing their voices had me crying tears of joy. It was good to be home.

I really took my camp experience to the max. I wrote about it and was worried for the second year. Yeah, I wanted to go again. I was happy when the camp told me that I was already with Brandon, Kyle, and Trent again. I sent them all letters except Jaron. Andrew was the only one who wrote back. His mom wrote that he'd return for camp in the first session, which wasn't good.

I went second session for this year and the next one. Still, I'd like to look at my first year of camp as an uplifting force. It was so powerful that I went another four times and am waiting for my sixth year. I've enjoyed revisiting this year because so much was missing in the original. These memories will last forever.

THE END!

The Camp: Season 2 Revisited
By Aaron Conn

When something goes really well, should you do it again? Well, it depends. When it comes to Summit Camp, I wanted to go again. I didn't want to go at first but after a great summer in 2004, I decided I would stay for the same amount of time. This year wasn't as good but like every year before and after, it was an experience. Like my 2005 essay on Season 1, the 2006 essay on Season 2 must be revisited. So with that, I'll try to revisit the summer of 2005.

It was July 26, 2005. My mom, my paternal grandmother, and I went to the same hotel that we went to almost a year ago. I was there because it was the start of second session at Summit Camp.

I remember crying when the time came to say goodbye. My mom spoke with two female counselors and they kept an eye on me for the trip up to camp. I kept myself occupied by watching the sci-fi cult classic television show, *Sliders*. I was watching this on my new portable DVD player. When we got to the camp, we got to the horseshoe.

There to pick me up was Kalyn, one of my new counselors. Ironically Kalyn was the younger sister of my female counselor from last year, Kenda. When I saw Kalyn, she was with one of my new bunkmates in B15 named Jim. Kalyn was showing him around. Brandon, from last year, was one of my bunkmates again. We talked a little and when I entered the bunk a familiar voice cried,

"Aaron!"

It was Kyle. I laughed and said hello. Also there was my friend, Trent. My new bunkmates, TJ and Colin, didn't say hello. It got to the point when it was too quiet. Luckily to break the silence, a black counselor who I saw on the porch came up to me and said,

"I got your e-mail. You said you'd bring movies?"

I said yes.

He looked through my collection and picked out my Queen DVD. Soon after he said,

"Oh, my name is Kelvin"

He then shook my hand. I figured he was Kelvin because I saw one counselor in the cabin sleeping. Like every bunk, we had name tags on our beds and hangers. On his bed, it read "Jono". This person turned out to be my third and final counselor Jonathan, aka Jono.

To my surprise, we went to hockey not too long after. During our lesson Alec from last year joined us. After hockey, we had showers. Last year on my first day, I didn't have to take a shower. Things changed this year and I took one.

After showers, I began to get anxious. I asked Jono if I could sit with him and Kelvin. He said I could and I tried to make the best of my time with them. During Horseshoe, I read my new book on Jim Morrison. The evening activity for that night was Movie Night. We watched *The Spongebob Squarepants Movie* and went to bed. I can remember as I was walking to the bathroom to get dressed I heard Kelvin say to Jono,

"So Brandon is moving to BST2 tomorrow…"

I thought I was hearing things and ignored it.

I woke up on Day 2 and saw that there was another counselor. It turned out to be our specialist, Brian. He would be working in computers this year. That morning, another camper moved into our bunk from BST2. His name was Jimmy and he would be taking Brandon's place (as there are two Jim's, I'll call the new one Jimmy to avoid confusion).

During AI, I had been building up all kinds of anxiety with swimming tests and Brandon moving out. I asked Kalyn if I could talk to her and right there, I cried. The pressure got to me. Kalyn helped by telling me that Andrew (from last year) was in B15 and had to move to the STs in the first session. She told me I'd be alright during the swimming test and I left it as that.

When the time came, I took my intermediate swimming test. It was so tense that I was running out of breath. That day was our picnic lunch so we chilled in the cabin. Kyle watched *Sliders* with me and it turned out that Brian liked the show as well. When informed that it would be raining periods five through seven, Kalyn told us that those periods were canceled. Brian played *Raiders of the Lost Ark* on his laptop to entertain us. I didn't like the movie and found it confusing. We also waitered for dinner.

As for an evening activity, we would be watching another movie on Brian's laptop. This time, it was the cult classic sci-fi film *Short Circuit*. However, Brandon had put me in a difficult situation. Apparently, he told a counselor named Jessica that I had a DVD player. Jessica was on OD (on duty) for that night. She asked if she could use it. At first, I told Kalyn to tell her no but when I found out we were watching *Short Circuit*, I changed my mind and let Jessica borrow my DVD player with the DVDs I had.

This was a bad move because once we went to bed; I didn't have my player back. I literally was up till midnight as I went to any door to find my DVD player. While on one porch, I found my third season set of *Sliders*. I grabbed it. In the end, counselors from B12 told me they'd talk to Kelvin.

Day 3, from what I wrote, was a good day. After breakfast, Brian had helped me get my DVD player and DVDs back. That day, sadly, saw us saying goodbye to Brandon as he left for BST2. I was upset but I just tried telling myself to not let this affect my year. On this day, it was trip day and it turned out that we would be going to the movies to see *The Adventures of Sharkboy and Lavagirl In 3D*. None of us were happy. During the movie, Trent and I hung out. As I predicted, the movie was a dud. Luckily, we had our first Splash Night.

Day 4 was a mixed day. We started off that day by canoeing down the Deleware River. I remember being in a canoe with Trent. I did note that Jimmy, Colin, and TJ didn't come. Everything was fine that day until during rest hour, TJ suddenly walked off. Something had gotten him pissed and he just walked away. This got me worried in how the bunk was getting along. That night was also International Night.

Day 5 wasn't easy. As Kalyn had the day off, it was Kelvin and Jono who were in charge that day. I didn't write a lot in my entry but what I did write about was the evening activity that night, which was Snatch the Flag night. I didn't participate because early on, I had spoken to Jono about my concerns with the tensions in the bunk. I then spoke to Kelvin in the cabin's bathroom. When I spoke with Kelvin, I cried. I can't remember what he said but whatever it was; it helped me get on with the rest of the day.

Day 6 was a good day. I said before that it was on this day that I felt the year sped right through. This was probably because I had my DVD player. On that day, Jim simply asked if he could watch *Sliders*. I told him he could and I'd watch it too. Trent later joined us and sometimes, Jono watched it. For the rest of the summer, we watched only certain episodes of the show. For this day, we watched two episodes. We also tried to watch the rest of *Short Circuit* but when the disc wouldn't play, we watched the sequel *Short Circuit 2*.

I didn't write a lot for Day 7. We had go-karts, computers, and poor periods of AI and swimming. In previous years, bunks were able to earn a bunk star for each period. The totals would be added up by Robbie G every Friday. This year, a new system started. Each period, bunks would have the chance to earn four bunk stars in four different areas. For those bad periods, we were given one and two stars. Other than that, Jim and I watch more *Sliders* when we went to the canteen and during showers.

Day 8 was the day we went hiking. Unlike last year when we spent the whole day hiking, we hiked for just four periods. At night, we finished up *Spongebob* and started *Are We There Yet?* At some point after, I spoke to Jono and then Kelvin about wanting to branch out and know more people in Karli's unit. Kelvin was proud so he gave me a hug and told me I could get out letters to all of them.

Looking back, this shows I was still anxious of making friends outside of my bunk. Day 9 was another short entry in my journal. I only noted that we had our weekly picnic lunch and that Trent, Jim, and I watch two episodes of *Sliders*.

Day 10 was another trip day. We went to Carousel Park, which was a small water park. My group was Kalyn, Trent, and Alec. The groups were very loose so we were all over the place because it was that small. During Horseshoe, I started to write my letters to the other bunks. We also had our splash night.

Day 11 was going great for the most part. We were getting perfect stars every period until last period in Ropes, we were given three stars. While we walked to the bunk, the bunk started to fight and blame each other on the reason why we didn't get perfect stars. Luckily Colin, Jimmy, and I were pulled away from it by Karli.

Karli told us that she had chosen us for Summit's Big Brother program. The older boys would come from both Karli or Dannelle's unit and the younger boys came from Pete's unit. The older boys were picked by the unit leaders. Karli probably thought I was mature so I was honored and hoped I got a good kid.

Meanwhile, Jono was picking shower order based on behavior. Jono let me go in next. Trent and Jim were already in there. I remember, jokingly, running inside away from all the tension outside.

The Big Brother program started on Day 12. My kid's name was Eli. We just walked and talked around the Horseshoe. Being the music listener I am, I asked him what music liked to listen to. He told me he liked pop and hip-hop music. I was a little thrown off and asked what TV shows and movies he liked to watch. He told me he liked *Kim Possible*. I thought it was going to be a disaster but in the end, it was nice to hang out with Eli.

That night was not good. We watched Brian's copy of *Batman Begins*, which was bootlegged as it wasn't on DVD yet. Due to the poor quality and advanced story, I couldn't understand it. Every time I asked what was happening, Kyle told me to shut up. Although I love the movie and its sequel (*The Dark Knight*) now, I gave up on the movie. I watched *The Bad News Bears* on my DVD player.

Accidently, the DVD player fell on the laptop and stopped both movies. With that, we went to bed. I can guess Kyle and others were pissed. Kelvin was also a bit angry at me as I hadn't gotten changed to go to bed yet, when he told everybody to have done so before the movie began. I took this too much to heart so I went outside and cried. The counselor on OD tried to calm me down and eventually, I went to bed.

Day 13 was Track and Field Day. B15 was on the White team. I remember finishing second place and the Red team finishing first. Still, it was sort of fun. I hated being forced to run for the track part on the AI field. I remember doing well but I think that might've been because I was with people who ran like me.

During Horseshoe that day, Trent and I wrote a song called "The Tension Song". Looking back, it's still a good song. I especially love the chorus but Trent only wrote a line in the song. I later used the song in 2009 for my concept album on camp, *Magic on the Hill*.

I only noted on Day 14 that I met Eli again and it was raining. Looking back at the original essay, I now remember that Trent was with me. After Horseshoe, I asked Trent what he thought of Eli. He said he didn't like him and he could tell that he didn't like me. I think this shows a future crack my friendship with Trent. I remember him being negative when it came to his thoughts on other people. If I can remember correctly the only people he liked during my three year tenure with him were Andrew, Brandon, Jim, and me until the incident in 2006.

Day 15 was the birthday of Maria, who did yoga that year. She was at our table so we got to have the brithday cake. That night, they finished up *Are We There Yet?* while Trent, Jim and I watched *Sliders*. During flashlight time, Kyle was bugging me so I could lend him my headphones. I told him no. He then made up this story that his mom had died and left a hidden message on the cassette he wanted to listen to, which was really a book-on-tape of *Eragon*. When I told him yes, I went outside and told either Jono or Kelvin to take care of Kyle.

Day 16 is a day I can't remember well. I noted that Trent got his own DVD player with his copy of *Monty Python and the Holy Grail*. I was jealous and wanting to continue *Sliders* but after a while, I figured it made sense to watch something new.

I also noted that Jimmy had a fit over a too-too, which was probably the most popular canteen treat. It was an ice cream cookie sandwich and that's what Jimmy was upset with. Jimmy had fits over a lot of things. This was just one of them. Day 17 was when we went to the Wayne County Fair. I was in a group with Brian and Jim.

Day 18 started off like any other day. The only difference was that all of us were missing our things such as tooth brushes and combs. We then found out that Alec had done something with our things. For the entire year, he wanted to go home. He was like this last year but this year, Alec could no longer handle Summit Camp. Out of his madness or depression, he went nuts yesterday. I remember him dumping a bucket of water on Brian during showers, which also ruined the chore wheel.

I was missing my brush/comb and according to Alec, he threw it out the window. Jono looked in the back of the cabin and said he found nothing. I remember Trent was really upset as he had lost everything. In the end, Alec was picked up by his parents and went home.

That night we saw the first part of the ST and GST play, *Star Wars*. It was horrible. Day 19 marked the demise of my DVD player. Before it broke, Jim, Trent, and I watched one episode. The second part of the *Star Wars* was suprisingly better than the first part.

Day 20 was the day that I tried out a reward system in the form of *Survivor*. I thought that each period, one camper would go due to bad behavior. This would be decided by the counselors but this day, it was decided by me. I'm not going to bother typing up the order but in the end, Trent won. We didn't do it again. You just can't play *Survivor* with a bunch of kids in it because feelings will get hurt. I was stupid and didn't see this as a problem.

Day 21 was the unit play for *Batman Begins*. It went really well as we all danced as a bunk. Kelvin was proud of the whole bunk. On Day 22, we saw the last two plays of *Spongebob* and *Westernly Ways*. Day 23 was our only day of perfect stars. During Clubs that night, I made B15 stick figures.

Day 24 was our last trip day. We went bowling and it was too funny. I had told the bunk how to "curse" the bowling bowl. Some of them believed it and I remember Jimmy throwing a fit and telling the counselors that Kyle and Colin were cursing his bowling ball! There was also a lottery game there which would come up every five minutes. This wasn't fair as Trent, Jim, TJ, and I had been bowling at the same rate. Every time, TJ came up for our lane. Kelvin was hilarous as he helped us stall the game. I remember winning once but the raffle didn't win me the prize in the end. Oh well!

Day 25 was the day we saw the staff play, *Mamma Mia!* It was okay. Trent also earned a CD case at the annual banquet for his three years. He gave me the case since he didn't own any CDs.

Day 26 was emotional. In the second session slideshow, I was in it three times. For the night, we were supposed to watch a VHS of *Monty Python's Flying Circus* I made. When all the TVs were taken, Brian played the movie *Teen Wolf* on his laptop.

On Day 27, it was really hard to say goodbye as always. Kyle and I went on the van/bus with my swimming instructor Lauren. I cried when I saw my mom and sister. It was good to be home.

Compared to the other summers I had at Summit, this one remains my least favorite. The problem with this year was that I had the DVD player, which took up a lot of the good times we could've been having.

However this year was still good as I met nice people, especially Kelvin. I saw him again from 2006 till 2008. This is also the year that inspired me to go for another year, which I had in mind in 2004. It also got me prepared for the next year, in which I started staying full session. Overall, my second year was good and revisiting a year I don't go back to often was really interesting.

THE END!

Counting Out Time: Days and Dates From *The Camp*
It's hard for me to keep track of when all these things in camp
happened. So, I label everyday as "Day #" and so forth. This is
simply a list of dates from each season. Enjoy!

Season 1- 2004
Day 1- July 27
Day 2- July 28
Day 3- July 29
Day 4- July 30
Day 5- July 31
Day 6- August 1
Day 7- August 2
Day 8- August 3
Day 9- August 4
Day 10- August 5
Day 11- August 6
Day 12- August 7
Day 13- August 8
Day 14- August 9
Day 15- August 10
Day 16- August 11
Day 17- August 12
Day 18- August 13
Day 19- August 14
Day 20- August 15
Day 21- August 16
Day 22- August 17
Day 23- August 18
Day 24- August 19
Day 25- August 20
Day 26- August 21

Day 27- August 22

Season 2- 2005
Day 1- July 26
Day 2- July 27
Day 3- July 28
Day 4- July 29
Day 5- July 30
Day 6- July 31
Day 7- August 1
Day 8- August 2
Day 9- August 3
Day 10- August 4
Day 11- August 5
Day 12- August 6
Day 13- August 7
Day 14- August 8
Day 15- August 9
Day 16- August 10
Day 17- August 11
Day 18- August 12
Day 19- August 13
Day 20- August 14
Day 21- August 15
Day 22- August 16
Day 23- August 17
Day 24- August 18
Day 25- August 19
Day 26- August 20
Day 27- August 21

Season 3- 2006
Day 1- June 29

Day 2- June 30
Day 3- July 1
Day 4- July 2
Day 5- July 3
Day 6- July 4
Day 7- July 5
Day 8- July 6
Day 9- July 7
Day 10- July 8
Day 11- July 9
Day 12- July 10
Day 13- July 11
Day 14- July 12
Day 15- July 13
Day 16- July 14
Day 17- July 15
Day 18- July 16
Day 19- July 17
Day 20- July 18
Day 21- July 19
Day 22- July 20
Day 23- July 21
Day 24- July 22
Day 25- July 23
Day 26- July 24
Day 27- July 25
Day 28- July 26
Day 29- July 27
Day 30- July 28
Day 31- July 29
Day 32- July 30
Day 33- July 31
Day 34- August 1
Day 35- August 2

Day 36- August 3
Day 37- August 4
Day 38- August 5
Day 39- August 6
Day 40- August 7
Day 41- August 8
Day 42- August 9
Day 43- August 10
Day 44- August 11
Day 45- August 12
Day 46- August 13
Day 47- August 14
Day 48- August 15
Day 49- August 16
Day 50- August 17
Day 51- August 18
Day 52- August 19
Day 53- August 20

Season 4- 2007
Day 1- June 21
Day 2- June 22
Day 3- June 23
Day 4- June 24
Day 5- June 25
Day 6- June 26
Day 7- June 27
Day 8- June 28
Day 9- June 29
Day 10- June 30
Day 11- July 1
Day 12- July 2
Day 13- July 3
Day 14- July 4

Day 15- July 5
Day 16- July 6
Day 17- July 7
Day 18- July 8
Day 19- July 9
Day 20- July 10
Day 21- July 11
Day 22- July 12
Day 23- July 13
Day 24- July 14
Day 25- July 15
Day 26- July 16
Day 27- July 17
Day 28- July 18
Day 29- July 19
Day 30- July 20
Day 31- July 21
Day 32- July 22
Day 33- July 23
Day 34- July 24
Day 35- July 25
Day 36- July 26
Day 37- July 27
Day 38- July 28
Day 39- July 29
Day 40- July 30
Day 41- July 31
Day 42- August 1
Day 43- August 2
Day 44- August 3
Day 45- August 4
Day 46- August 5
Day 47- August 6
Day 48- August 7

Day 49- August 8
Day 50- August 9
Day 51- August 10
Day 52- August 11
Day 53- August 12

<u>Season 5- 2008</u>
Day 1- June 26
Day 2- June 27
Day 3- June 28
Day 4- June 29
Day 5- June 30
Day 6- July 1
Day 7- July 2
Day 8- July 3
Day 9- July 4
Day 10- July 5
Day 11- July 6
Day 12- July 7
Day 13- July 8
Day 14- July 9
Day 15- July 10
Day 16- July 11
Day 17- July 12
Day 18- July 13
Day 19- July 14
Day 20- July 15
Day 21- July 16
Day 22- July 17
Day 23- July 18
Day 24- July 19
Day 25- July 20
Day 26- July 21
Day 27- July 22

Day 28- July 23
Day 29- July 24
Day 30- July 25
Day 31- July 26
Day 32- July 27
Day 33- July 28
Day 34- July 29
Day 35- July 30
Day 36- July 31
Day 37- August 1
Day 38- August 2
Day 39- August 3
Day 40- August 4
Day 41- August 5
Day 42- August 6
Day 43- August 7
Day 44- August 8
Day 45- August 9
Day 46- August 10
Day 47- August 11
Day 48- August 12
Day 49- August 13
Day 50- August 14

Season 6- 2009
Day 1- June 24
Day 2- June 25
Day 3- June 26
Day 4- June 27
Day 5- June 28
Day 6- June 29
Day 7- June 30
Day 8- July 1
Day 9- July 2

Day 10- July 3
Day 11- July 4
Day 12- July 5
Day 13- July 6
Day 14- July 7
Day 15- July 8
Day 16- July 9
Day 17- July 10
Day 18- July 11
Day 19- July 12
Day 20- July 13
Day 21- July 14
Day 22- July 15
Day 23- July 16
Day 24- July 17
Day 25- July 18
Day 26- July 19
Day 27- July 20
Day 28- July 21
Day 29- July 22
Day 30- July 23
Day 31- July 24
Day 32- July 25
Day 33- July 26
Day 34- July 27
Day 35- July 28
Day 36- July 29
Day 37- July 30
Day 38- July 31
Day 39- August 1
Day 40- August 2
Day 41- August 3
Day 42- August 4
Day 43- August 5

Day 44- August 6
Day 45- August 7
Day 46- August 8
Day 47- August 9
Day 48- August 10

Acknowledgements

I would like to take the moment to thank a few people who've helped me make this book happen or anything happen in my life.

I would like to thank all 55 groupmates/bunkmates that I've been with from 2004 to 2009. Even if there are those of you who hate me (most likely, I feel the same), you made my years at camp and travel what they are.

I'd also like to thank all 18 counselors I had from 2004 to 2009. You've been there when I needed help. I also want to include all the specialists, unit leaders, mentors, and directors who've also been there as well.

Also, I'd like to thank all of my family for believing in me and supporting my career as a journalist. Special thanks to my mom, who helped check for grammatical errors in all of the essays in this book.

Lastly, I want to dedicate this book to those people who aren't living anymore. This includes my dad and Tim Kedge. Rest in peace and God bless both of you!

Remembering Tim Kedge

As the last part of this 10th anniversary edition of *The Camp*, I would like to mention something that I should have mentioned in the first edition.

I've spoke many times about the late great Tim Kedge. He truly was a remarkable man and I still look up to him. Every March 31st and June 2nd (his death date and his birth date), I spend some time to remember this wonderful man. The thing I did not mention was as to how Tim passed away. Unfortunately, Tim died after a rather short battle with leukemia.

One of the great things about getting a book out is that you get paid for all your hard work. I thought to myself what I would do with this money. What use could come of it? After working on something like this for such a long time, I felt like I couldn't take the money. I just can't spend it.

Soon enough, the idea came to me: I decided all the money I made from this book would towards leukemia research. The sad thing is that the campers really didn't get to have a memorial or anything to remember Tim by when he passed. I feel this is the best I can do to show how much I loved this man.

Unfortunately, the checks I did get for the first edition for this book just disappeared. I feel really bad that I haven't been able to donate anything. So I'm going to give this another try.

Portions of your money that you used to purchase this book will go towards research that can probably save some lives.

Thank you for reading and purchasing this book.

Aaron Conn
February 26, 2014

www.ingramcontent.com/pod-product-compliance
Lightning Source LLC
La Vergne TN
LVHW011228080426
835509LV00005B/372